BIOLOGY
Revision Guide for CSEC® Examinations

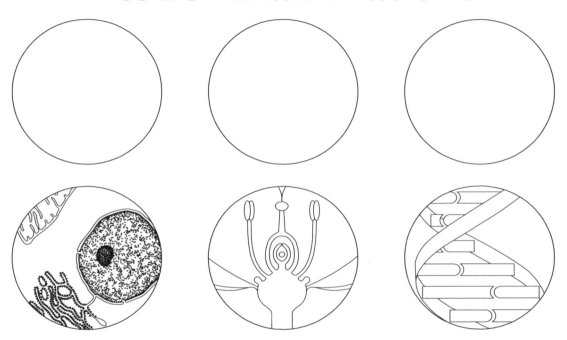

Eugenie Williams, Cheryl-Anne Gayle and Roland Soper

CAMBRIDGE
UNIVERSITY PRESS

CAMBRIDGE UNIVERSITY PRESS
Cambridge, New York, Melbourne, Madrid, Cape Town,
Singapore, São Paulo, Delhi, Mexico City

Cambridge University Press
The Edinburgh Building, Cambridge CB2 8RU, UK

www.cambridge.org
Information on this title: www.cambridge.org/9780521692953

First published 1987
Second edition 2009
Reprinted 2013

Printed in the United Kingdom by Printondemand-worldwide, Peterborough

A catalogue record for this publication is available from the British Library

ISBN 978-0-521-69295-3 Paperback

Editor: Sandra Cattich
Typesetter: Charlene Bate
Illustrators: Andrew Kerr, James Whitelaw
Proofreader: Bridget Farham
Indexer: Jeanne Cope

Contents

Introduction – preparation for examinations

Your school or private institution will enter you for the examination. Otherwise you should make your own arrangements.

1. Obtain a syllabus to help you with your revision and provide information on the format of the examination.
2. Obtain recent copies of the specimen papers for the examination and past examination papers.
3. Work out a programme of revision and allow for steady coverage during a period of 6–8 weeks before the first date of the examination.
4. Revise for short periods of 1–2 hours and then have a rest, go for a walk or try some other relaxation. Then return for another session of work, feeling refreshed. Do not attempt to concentrate for long periods.
5. To achieve this programme of work you need to be fit. Take regular exercise, go to bed early and keep regular hours. Do not smoke, take alcohol or use drugs (except those prescribed by a doctor).

Revision hints

1. Try to **work on your own** without any distractions such as music, television or the conversation of people. Create an environment similar to that in the exam room.
2. **Sit at a well-lit table** with your books and really work for the time suggested above. Do not sit in an easy chair or lie down. Remember that learning can be enjoyable but it is also hard work.
3. At this stage, it is important to **concentrate on the essential points**. The objective is to learn facts, understand principles, theories, and above all, to retain these throughout the examination period.

Methods of learning

Use varied techniques to learn the concepts to be covered:

1. **Read** or **recite** the material aloud.
2. **Write out** the material in note form, preferably in point form on index or note cards.
3. **Practise drawing** diagrams, flow charts, natural cycles and so on.
4. **Work through examination questions** by writing out the answers. Always check the answers if you are not sure; consult with your teacher.
5. **Revise topic by topic** using your notes and using this book.

Before the examination

1. On the night before the examination get to bed early.
2. Check (and recheck) the paper number, starting time and examination venue.
3. Make sure that you have all the writing and other instruments that you require. Put black or blue ink pens, pencils, a ruler, protractor, compass, eraser and pencil sharpener into a clear plastic bag.
4. Be sure that you know your **centre name** and **number** and your own **personal candidate number**. Have these written on a piece of paper with your instruments. Remember that both centre and candidate number must be written at the top of each answer booklet, each page of writing paper and each answer sheet.

The examination day

1. Allow **plenty of time** to reach the examination centre. Get up early and have a good breakfast.
2. **Check all the instruments** you are taking to the examination.
3. Allow extra time to get to the examination hall in case of traffic jams or other delays.
4. Wait outside the examination hall until called in by the invigilator.
5. Make sure that you have **your identification card**, school pass or whatever means of identification is required.
6. **Go to your assigned seat** (usually numbered with your examination number).
7. Fill in the **answer booklet or sheet** when it is given out and you are told to start.
8. **Read the instructions** very carefully and follow them closely. These instructions will establish:
   a the time allowance;
   b the number of questions to be answered; and
   c whether there is question choice.
   The time allowed to read the paper from start to finish is indicated on the paper. Divide the remaining time by the number of questions to give you an idea of how much time to spend on each question.
9. When **end of time** is indicated you are to **put down your pen**. It is essential therefore that five minutes before the end of the examination you ensure that:
   a all your papers are headed with your candidate number;

b your papers are in the correct order and numbered;

c no papers have become mixed with your rough work and likewise no rough work is mixed in with your papers.

Do not write anything after you are told to stop.

Types of question

You will find examples of each type of question to be asked illustrated in this book. Read all instructions written on the front of the question booklet of each of the papers. They are as follows:

Paper 1: 1 hour 15 minutes – 60 multiple-choice or objective-type questions

Paper 2: 1 hour 30 minutes – five compulsory structured questions including one data-analysis question

Paper 3: 1 hour 10 minutes – six essay-type questions, grouped in pairs, which are arranged in three sections: A, B and C. Answer one question from each section: a total of three questions.

Paper 1: 1 hour 15 minutes – 60 multiple-choice or objective-type questions

Each test question has four suggested answers, which are lettered (A), (B), (C) and (D). **Read each question carefully**. You need to choose the best answer, but try to answer the statement or problem before looking at the answer choices. Select the correct answer by eliminating the choices that you think are incorrect and focus on the other choices.

Answer the questions you find easier first; skip harder questions and place a mark next to the number on the answer sheet. Do not waste time puzzling over one question that stumps you; move on and come back to it later. On multiple-choice papers your first answer is usually the correct one; do not second guess yourself and change your response.

Example:
The best method of preventing the spread of disease by an insect vector is to:
(A) screen windows or doors;
(B) kill adult insects by spraying with insecticides;
(C) vaccinate against disease;
(D) destroy the insect's eggs and larvae.

Notice that all these answers are possible methods, but you are asked to select the 'best' method. Only answer

(D) will ensure that no adult insects develop and are around to bite humans. Answers (A) to (C) could help but would not kill the vectors at their source.

Paper 2: 1 hour 30 minutes – five compulsory structured questions including one data-analysis question

Answer all parts of the questions; do not leave any blank spaces. It is recommended that you spend no more than 30 minutes on Question 1, which is the **data–analysis** question: **do it first**. The data will be of various types e.g. **diagrams, graphs, tables or statements**.

Data-analysis questions often involve the construction of line graphs, histograms, bar and pie charts. Remember the following:

1 Choose scales on the graph paper that will fill it.
2 The horizontal axis should represent the *variable* controlled by the *experimenter* (e.g. temperature, time).
3 The vertical axis should represent the *variable* under *investigation* (e.g. changes in mass, height).
4 Axes must be labelled (e.g. Mass (g)) and the units entered along the axes (e.g. 0, 2, 4, 6, 8).
5 Enter the points in pencil as 'x' or as small encircled dots.
6 Points should be joined appropriately (i.e. using either a smooth curve or a straight line).

Answer subsequent questions in the order of your choice starting with those you find the easiest. Pay attention to **keywords**, these are usually underlined, in capital letters, or in bold type. Answers are to be brief, concise, to the point, and written in the spaces provided. A word or short phrase is usually adequate for several questions on this paper. Provide only relevant information. Avoid repeating the question or parts of the question as a preamble to your answer – this wastes time and space.

Example:
State **one** disadvantage of using artificial fertilisers. A poorly structured response may be: 'One disadvantage of artificial fertilisers is that the soil becomes acidic in time'. A better response would be, 'Soil becomes acidic in time'. Write only on the lines provided. **Do not write in the margins**, and **do not add extra lines**.

Paper 3: 1 hour 10 minutes – six essay-type questions, grouped in pairs and arranged in three sections A, B and C

Each question may be further subdivided into parts. Answer **one** from each pair. In your 10 minutes reading time there must be no writing in your answer booklet, but you can write on the question paper using a pencil. Choose the questions you will answer carefully. Be sure you can answer ALL the parts of the question.

Underline key words, plan your response, and jot down relevant terms or words that come to mind. You should spend no more than 20 minutes on each question in this paper.

Be sure that you use the appropriate biological terminology – correct spelling is important. Include drawings, where useful, to assist your description of biological processes or structures as required.

Guidelines for biology drawings

1 Draw with a sharpened HB pencil.
2 Large, clearly labelled drawings with space on both sides for labels are essential. Labels are to be written in capital or common letters only. Label lines must be drawn with a pencil and ruler; the lines must touch the structures that they are to identify.
3 Include a title below your drawing, which includes the name of the structure, the view or type of section, i.e. T.S. (transverse section) or C.S. (cross section) or L.S. (longitudinal section).
4 If a question requires you to **use annotated diagrams only** do remember that annotations are brief notes written next to the labels that state the function of the structure labelled or another feature that the diagram does not show, such as texture or colour.

In this paper you can expect that your awareness of the social, economic and environmental implications of biology in human daily activity, science, agriculture, medicine and industry will be tested. Your comments or suggestions in response to questions of this nature must present a well-reasoned, balanced view, based on biological facts and concepts as well as currently accepted theory.

Terms used in questions on examination papers

Knowing the meaning of the following terms used in questions on examination papers will help you to correctly interpret what the Examiner expects from you:
Annotated drawing or **diagrams** – a large labelled drawing or diagram is required and, alongside each label, a brief description of the function of each part.
Comment – state opinion or view with supporting reasons.

Compare – state the similarities and differences.
Define – state concisely the meaning of the word or term.
Describe – provide detailed factual information on the appearance or arrangement of a specific structure or the sequence of a specific process.
Discuss – give details and, if relevant, the positive and negative points of a subject as well as evidence for these positions; present a reasoned argument giving valid points both for and against.
Distinguish – concentrate on the differences between or among items that can be used to define them or place them into separate categories.
Draw – make a line representation that shows the accurate relationship between the parts – all drawings must be labelled.
Explain or account for – give reasons based on your accurate recall of biological concepts.
Give an illustrated account of … or **With the use of diagrams …** – give a written description, which includes diagrams.
List – itemise, without detail, a series of points or observations.
Name – give the name only, no further information is required.
Outline – requires a description of the most important points or basic steps only.
State – provide factual information in concise terms, omitting detailed explanations.
Suggest – offer an explanation based on the information presented and your knowledge of biology.

Diagrams to memorise

You must be able to draw and label the following from memory:

1 The nitrogen and carbon cycle
2 Animal and plant cells to show: cell wall, cell membrane, nucleus, cytoplasm, mitochondria, vacuoles and chloroplasts
3 A dicotyledonous (dicot) leaf – external features and transverse section
4 The human digestive system
5 The internal structure of a tooth
6 Human gas exchange system and simple line drawings to show the behaviour of the rib cage and diaphragm during inhalation and exhalation
7 A longitudinal section through the heart
8 A transverse section through blood vessels – artery, vein and capillary
9 A plan diagram to show the blood vessels supplying the major organs
10 Blood cells – red, white, platelets
11 A transverse section of a dicotyledonous stem to show the arrangement of vascular tissue

1 Living organisms in the environment

[syllabus sections A1.1; 2.1 to 2.7]

Living organisms are best studied in a natural habitat but many animals can be collected and studied in the laboratory and then (if possible) returned to their habitat. Plants should never be dug up and taken to a laboratory or garden. Take only samples of leaves, flowers and fruit. One must always ensure that natural **ecosystems** (plants and animals in a natural community) are preserved. Selected samples of plants and animals can be collected as **specimens** for work in classification and ecology.

Let's have a look at the different ways in which we can classify living organisms.

1.1 Natural classification

Natural classification is the arrangement of living organisms into groups based on overall similarities. The more features organisms have in common, the closer their evolutionary relationships.

Basically, there are five major **kingdoms**; they are Prokaryotes, Protoctista, Fungi, Plants, and Animals (see Fig. 1.1 below). Each kingdom can be divided into **phyla** (singular phylum). Each phylum has major sub-groups called **classes**. Each class is sub-divided into **orders**, orders into **families**, and families into **genera** and **species**. Table 1.1 shows the classification of humans.

Binomial nomenclature was developed by Carolus Linnaeus. It is a method of naming plants and animals using two Latin names: the first being the genus and the second the species. Thus *Panthera leo* (the lion) is one species while *Panthera tigris* (the tiger) is another species of the same genus.

Table 1.1 *The classification of humans*

Kingdom	Animal
Phylum	Chordata
Class	Mammalia
Order	Primates
Family	Hominidae
Genus	*Homo*
Species	*sapiens*

1.2 Feeding modes

Living organisms can be placed into two main groups according to their mode of nutrition:
- **Autotrophs** (producers) – synthesise complex organic compounds from simple inorganic compounds (they require an energy source to do this); and
- **Heterotrophs** (consumers) – obtain their required organic compounds by feeding on autotrophs.

(Insectivorous plants use both heterotrophic and autotrophic modes of nutrition.)

Autotrophs can be divided into two further groups:
- **Photoautotrophs** – those autotrophs that use light as a source of energy for the synthesis of organic compounds (e.g. green plants); and
- **Chemoautotrophs** – those autotrophs that obtain energy from chemical reactions to make complex organic molecules (e.g. nitrifying bacteria – see Fig. 2.2 The nitrogen cycle on p. 8).

Fig. 1.1 *The five-kingdom system of classification*

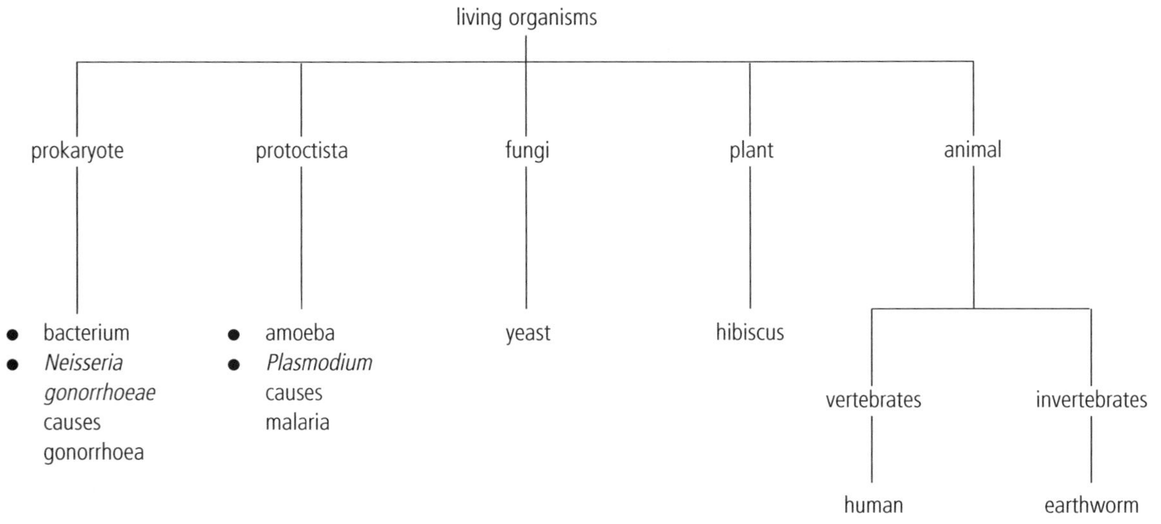

Heterotrophs can be divided into three further groups:
- **Holozoic organisms** – those heterotrophs that ingest complex organic molecules and digest these to small soluble molecules, which they then use (e.g. mammals);
- **Saprophytic organisms** – those heterotrophs that secrete digestive enzymes onto organic material (parts of, or entire organisms) and absorb the simple molecules produced by the activity of the enzymes into their bodies (e.g. fungi such as *Mucor* (common mould) and *Rhizopus* (bread mould) and bacteria, which are also responsible for the decay of organic material; and
- **Parasitic organisms** – those heterotrophs that live on or in another living organism and obtain food from these organisms (which we call hosts, e.g. bacteria, fleas, love vine, tapeworms).

1.3 Feeding relationships

The following terms describe feeding relationships in the food chain, providing another way of classifying organisms.

Producer – an autotroph (e.g. plants on land and phytoplankton in aquatic environments).

Herbivore – a plant-eating animal (e.g. sheep).

Carnivore – a flesh-eating animal (e.g. shark).

Omnivore – an animal that eats both plants and animals (e.g. humans).

Consumer – herbivores and carnivores are consumers in that they are heterotrophs, which obtain their nutrition from producers.

Predator – any animal that hunts, captures and kills other animals (which we call their prey). Since they kill animals for food, predators are also carnivores (e.g. praying mantises). In a predator-prey relationship, the prey are ideally present in larger numbers than the predator, though the populations of each fluctuate.

Food chain – a feeding relationship between organisms in an environment. The chain begins with producers that trap light energy, converting it to chemical energy. The producers are eaten by primary consumers (herbivores) and these are eaten by

secondary consumers. There may be tertiary consumers giving a four-link food chain. The tertiary consumer is sometimes called a top carnivore.

Trophic level – each stage of a food chain is called a trophic level.

Biological equilibrium – this occurs when the numbers of producers and consumers are balanced in a population. The fluctuating numbers of the predator-prey relationship are not in complete equilibrium, but the mean (average) numbers remain constant in what we call **dynamic equilibrium**.

Decomposer – saprophytic microorganisms (bacteria and fungi) that bring about decay. These form an important part of food chains, particularly in the recycling of mineral elements, which they make available for plants. Decomposers are found at all trophic levels since all organisms die and decay.

Food web – a number of food chains that are interconnected.

Energy flow – represents the vital importance of food chains and food webs. All life requires energy and all energy originates from the light of the sun. Green plants incorporate energy. The compounds containing this pass from organism to organism through the food chain, being used and lost in living processes (see Fig. 1.3). In food chains involving humans (e.g.

corn ⟶ cattle ⟶ human), only about 0.5% of the energy of sunlight incorporated into the corn plant reaches humans who consume meat. People would obtain more energy per unit mass of the food if they ate the maize.

Current definitions of relationships between organisms are based on the physical **closeness** of organisms relative to each other:
- **Symbiosis** – is defined as the **close** physical interaction between organisms of different species in which both derive benefit e.g. nitrogen-fixing bacteria living in the root nodules of a legume: the plant gets nitrogen from the bacteria and the bacteria get carbohydrates from the plant. Symbiosis is a form of mutualism.

Table 1.2 *Trophic levels*

Trophic level	Food chains		Nutritional classification	Mode of feeding
	Aquatic	*Terrestrial*		
4	Large fish	Bird	Tertiary consumer (carnivore)	Heterotrophic
3	Small fish	Lizard	Secondary consumer (carnivore)	Heterotrophic
2	Shrimp	Cricket	Primary consumer (herbivore)	Heterotrophic
1	Phytoplankton	Pea plant	Producer	Autotrophic

- **Commensalism** – one species gains and the other is unaffected e.g. cattle egrets following cattle can pick up insects disturbed by the cattle moving through a pasture.
- **Mutualism** – may not necessarily involve **close** physical contact. Insects, e.g. bees, feeding on the nectar get a supply of food from flowers, while the flowers benefit from the fact that bees transfer their pollen from one flower to another. Both species therefore benefit.

- **Parasitism** – organisms that live in or on another organism (the host), which often suffers some adverse effect. Many bacteria and all viruses are parasites causing symptoms of disease in the host. Single-celled organisms (protozoa) are sometimes parasites. An example is *Plasmodium*, an internal parasite that lives in the human red blood cell and causes malaria. Fleas are external parasites of dogs and cats. A successful parasite never causes the death of its host.

Fig. 1.2 *Food web of organisms in the sea*

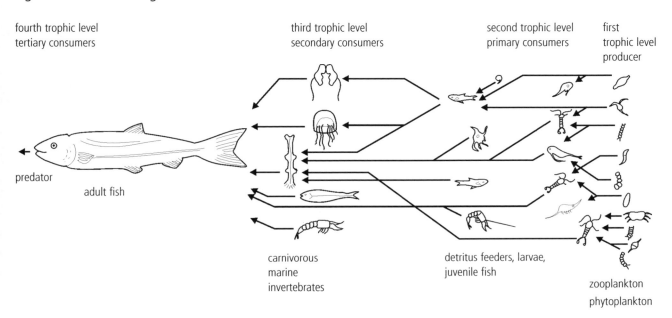

fourth trophic level
tertiary consumers

third trophic level
secondary consumers

second trophic level
primary consumers

first trophic level
producer

predator

adult fish

carnivorous marine invertebrates

detritus feeders, larvae, juvenile fish

zooplankton
phytoplankton

Fig. 1.3 *Energy flow through a food chain*

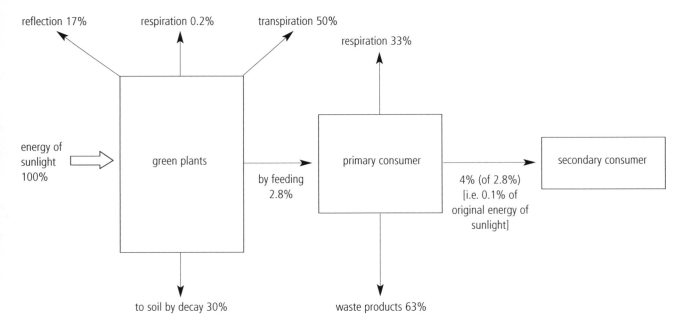

reflection 17%

respiration 0.2%

transpiration 50%

respiration 33%

energy of sunlight 100%

green plants

primary consumer

secondary consumer

by feeding 2.8%

4% (of 2.8%) [i.e. 0.1% of original energy of sunlight]

to soil by decay 30%

waste products 63%

2 Nutrient cycling

Mineral elements are constantly re-used or recycled in natural environments (e.g. carbon and nitrogen). Decomposers, symbiotic bacteria and fungi are very important to carbon and nitrogen cycles.

2.1 The carbon cycle

The carbon cycle refers to the circulation of carbon atoms in carbon compounds between living organisms and their environment (see Fig. 2.1).

Fig. 2.1 *The carbon cycle*

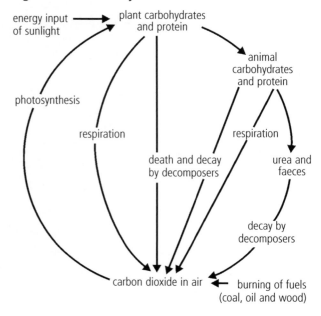

2.2 The nitrogen cycle

The nitrogen cycle refers to the circulation of nitrogen atoms as gas or within nitrogen compounds in nature (see Fig. 2.2).

Bacteria involved in the nitrogen cycle

Nitrogen-fixing bacteria – convert free nitrogen to nitrates.
1 *Rhizobium* – symbiotic bacteria living in the root nodules of leguminous plants (e.g. pea, bean). They obtain carbohydrates, used as a source of energy, from the plant. The plant receives nitrogen compounds in return.
2 *Azotobacter* – non-symbiotic bacteria living in the soil, needing aerobic conditions.
3 *Clostridium* – non-symbiotic bacteria living in the soil in anaerobic conditions.

Fig. 2.2 *The nitrogen cycle*

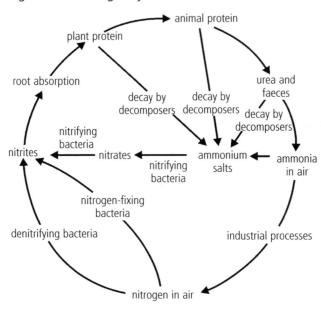

Nitrifying bacteria – live in the soil; convert ammonia and ammonium compounds to nitrites and then nitrites to nitrates.
1 *Nitrosomonas* – convert ammonia and ammonium compounds to nitrites.
2 *Nitrobacter* – convert nitrites to nitrates.
Nitrosomonas and *Nitrobacter* are chemosynthetic bacteria. During the oxidation of ammonia and nitrites, energy is released. This energy is used to synthesise simple organic compounds.

Denitrifying bacteria – usually live in soil that is lacking in oxygen, such as waterlogged soils. They break down nitrates and nitrites to obtain oxygen. These bacteria therefore reduce soil fertility by reducing the amount of nitrogen available to plant roots.

2.3 Energy flow through living organisms

Energy is incorporated into green plants and then passed on through food chains from herbivores to carnivores. These organisms eventually die and can be eaten by scavengers or simply rot away due to the action of decomposers (see Fig. 2.3). Note that while energy moves from one organism to the next with associated losses, mineral elements can be recycled.

Fig. 2.3 *The cycle of compounds and the flow of energy*

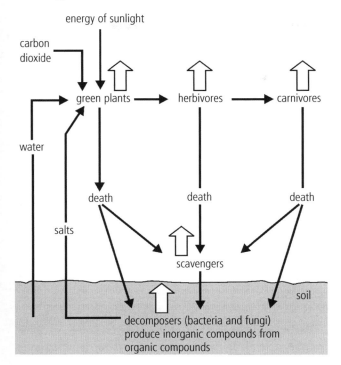

2.4 The interdependence of plant and animal life

1 Plants synthesise all food for animals by photosynthesis.
2 During photosynthesis, plants use carbon dioxide and give off large quantities of oxygen, which is used by animals.
3 During respiration animals give off carbon dioxide that is used by plants for photosynthesis.
4 The death of plants and animals returns mineral salts to the soil that can be used again by plants.
5 Plants can use nitrogenous animal wastes.

3 The environment and man

3.1 Some terms

Environment – the sum total of all of the conditions in which an organism lives i.e. the organic or biotic factors (other living organisms needed for food i.e. prey, predators and decomposers) and the inorganic abiotic factors (i.e. light, temperature, relative humidity, rainfall, soil).

Habitat – the particular area in which an organism lives – e.g. the seashore, ponds (aquatic habitats) or woodland, grassland (terrestrial habitats).

Niche – all of the environmental conditions and resources needed for an organism to survive, reproduce and maintain a viable population.

Population – a group of organisms of the same species that live in a particular area or habitat.

Community – a collection of different populations occupying the same habitat. It can range from very large (tropical rain forest) to very small (under a stone in a garden). Large communities contain many small communities within them.

Ecosystem – one or more communities of organisms, in a specific habitat, together with the inorganic components of that habitat such as a pond or a large tree.

3.2 Factors affecting the distribution of organisms

Abiotic or physical factors

Temperature

Organisms will survive in environments where the temperature ranges are within that to which the organism is physically and metabolically suited. Temperature affects the enzyme activity within the organism and therefore also affects metabolism.

Temperatures in terrestrial habitats vary more than in aquatic habitats.

Wind

Allows for the dispersal of seeds and fruits, so allowing organisms to colonise more habitats. However, high winds can damage plants, tearing foliage or toppling plants with shallow roots.

Light intensity

Light is extremely important in any ecosystem. Autotrophs, and so consequently all other organisms, require it. Plants in particular need varying amounts of light e.g. the trees, shrubs, herbs, ferns and mosses, which form clearly defined layers in a tropical rain forest. Seasonal and daily variations affect photosynthesis and transpiration in plants and vitamin D synthesis in humans.

Rainfall

The amount of water received determines the character of the large ecosystems throughout the world, from deserts to forests. Tropical rainforests develop in areas where temperature and rainfall are high. Where there is less rainfall only grasses can develop. Cacti and succulents grow where water is limited.

Humidity

Relative humidity is a measure of the amount of water in the atmosphere. This is a very important factor that influences the distribution of small organisms that have thin outer coverings and that are at risk of drying out in conditions of low humidity, e.g. woodlice under damp wood or earthworms in moist soil.

Edaphic factors

Soil forms an important link between the biotic and abiotic components of terrestrial habitats. Soil conditions such as pH, salinity, and mineral components, organic matter, air content and water content influence plant growth and the distribution of soil organisms.

Biotic factors

The abiotic (physical) factors play a very important part in the distribution of living organisms within an ecosystem, but biotic factors can also have an important effect. The most influential are human activities such as agriculture, forestry, the building of cities, residential communities and the making of roads. These all destroy natural ecosystems. Animals can affect plant communities by grazing, browsing, trampling the vegetation (e.g. large herds of goats can completely destroy herbs and shrubs in a community). Plants can also affect other plants (e.g. large trees produce considerable shade in which no other plants can grow).

4 Soil

4.1 Soil components

Soil is formed by weathering (the action of water, wind, frost and ice) on rocks. It consists of particles surrounded by water and air spaces. The crumb structure relates to the size of the particles, i.e. sand, clay and silt, together with the amount of **humus** present. Humus is made of decaying plant and animal remains.

The relative proportions of sand, silt and clay determine soil texture. Clays, clay loams and silt loams are most suitable for plant growth. Loams consist of equal quantities of clay and sand with some intermediate particles.

4.2 Soil fauna and flora

Animals constitute the soil fauna while plants form the soil flora (micro-organisms such as bacteria and fungi). Together soil fauna and flora form food chains and food webs with herbivores and carnivores – all supported by decaying plant material. As a result of the *desirable* inter-relationships and activities of these soil organisms, there is:

1   decay of organic matter;
2   release of mineral salts for plant uptake;
3   formation of the appropriate soil structure;
4   breakdown of chemicals and substances (bio-degradable activity);
5   increased aeration and drainage; and
6   fixation of atmospheric nitrogen for use by plants.

Table 4.1 *Properties of sand and clay*

Property	Sand	Clay
Texture	Coarse, particles >0.2 mm	Fine, particles <0.002 mm
Porosity	Large pore spaces, well aerated, drains quickly	Small pore spaces, poor aeration, drains slowly
Water-holding capacity	Poor retention, water not held by capillarity, does not become waterlogged	Good water retention, water held by capillarity and forms a film around clay particles, becomes waterlogged easily, cracks when dry, clumps when wet
Nutrient retention	Low, mineral elements rapidly leached out so that soil becomes acidic	High, not leached, clay particles attract mineral ions

The soil organisms, however, do have *undesirable* activities that may decrease the fertility. They:

1   change available nitrates into nitrogen;
2   compete with crop plants for nutrients;
3   cause injury and disease to root structures; and
4   cause damage and so reduce productivity of crops.

Table 4.2 *Components of soil*

Component	Constituents	Function
Rock particles	Insoluble – gravel, sand, clay, silt and volcanic ash	Soil framework for binding and retention of all other components
Mineral salts	Soluble – compounds of nitrogen, potassium, magnesium, phosphorus, calcium	Provide essential elements in the compounds, e.g. ammonium nitrate, calcium nitrate, calcium phosphate, magnesium, calcium carbonate
Air	Soil air containing oxygen and nitrogen	(i) Oxygen for respiration of plant roots and soil organisms (ii) Nitrogen for nitrogen-fixing bacteria forming nitrogen compounds
Water	Received from rain downwards – upward seepage from under-ground sources i.e. capillarity	(i) Dissolves mineral salts (ii) Absorbed for photosynthesis (iii) Absorbed for plant turgidity (iv) Dissolves nutrients produced by soil organisms
Bacteria and fungi	Bacteria and fungi, including nitrifying, denitrifying and nitrogen-fixing bacteria	(i) Break down organic material forming humus (ii) Form nitrates from ammonium compounds (iii) Fix atmospheric nitrogen
Other living organisms	Worms, arthropods, molluscs	Feed on plant material forming complex food webs. Improve drainage, aeration – their dead bodies contribute more organic material for breakdown to produce salts
Humus	Dead and decaying plants and animals	(i) Provides salts (ii) Retains water (iii) Binds the soil particles

5 Studying an ecosystem

In order to analyse the organisms living in a given habitat, the community structure must be determined. It is not possible to find and count all of the animals and plants, so sampling techniques have been developed to indicate the species present and the numbers involved.

5.1 Sampling of plants

Line transect

A line transect is a tape or string that is run along the ground between two sticks. The plant species that actually touch the string are identified and recorded in a field notebook.

Fig. 5.1 *(a) Setting out a line transect for ground flora (b) Positioning of quadrats along a line transect*

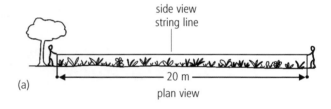

(a)

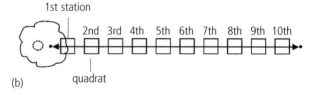

(b)

Belt transect

A belt transect is a strip of chosen width across the habitat, made by setting up two line transects, say 1 m apart. Another method is to use a line transect and then a quadrat frame spaced along it (see below). In both methods the plant species are recorded along the line of the belt transect.

Quadrat

A quadrat is a frame (wood or metal) that forms a square of known area (0.25 m² or 1 m²). The species within the frame can be recorded. A quadrat may be used without a transect in order to obtain a random sample of an area. This is done by throwing the quadrat in a random fashion and recording the species within it each time it falls.

Fig. 5.2 *Quadrat frame (1 m²) with wire sub-quadrats (each 400 cm²) forming a graduated quadrat*

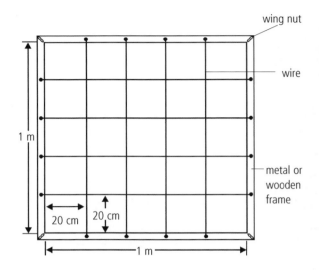

5.2 Sampling of animals

Nets

Various types of net can be used according to the type of habitat, e.g. trees or water. A sweep net consists of a nylon net attached to a handle that can be swept through grass and bushes to catch insects and spiders. Plankton nets have very fine mesh with a small jar or bottle attached to the rear of the net. This can be swept through water to catch minute floating animals and plants.

Fig. 5.3 *(a) Sweep net for use in land or water habitats (b) Plankton net for floating organisms in water (c) Specimen bottles*

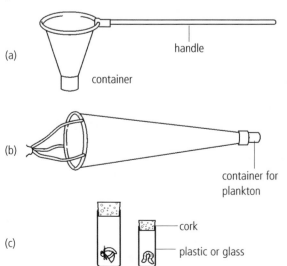

Beating tray

A beating tray is simply a sheet of fabric of known area held under a branch of a tree or shrub, which is beaten with a stick. The organisms fall into the sheet and can be collected.

Pooter

A pooter is an apparatus used to collect small organisms from a beating tray or net (see Fig. 5.4).

Fig. 5.4 *A pooter for collecting small organisms*

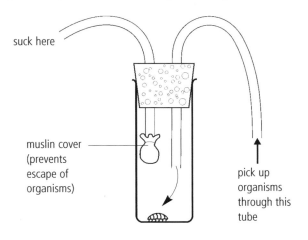

suck here

muslin cover
(prevents
escape of
organisms)

pick up
organisms
through this
tube

5.3 Estimating population size

In all population studies it is essential to be able to estimate the number of organisms within a given area of the habitat (ground or water). The methods employed are determined by the size and mode of life of the organisms.

There are three aspects of species distribution that can be calculated:

1 **Species density**: the number of members of a given species within a given area e.g. 10 m^2 (obtained by randomly thrown quadrats);

2 **Species frequency**: a measure of the chance of finding a given species with any one throw of a quadrat (if a species is found only once in ten throws of a quadrat it has a frequency of 10%);

3 **Species cover**: the proportion of ground covered by any one species, so that it can finally give the area covered by the species as a percentage of the total area. A metre square quadrat is used and an estimate is made for each species within the frame.

6 Natural populations

[syllabus sections E3.1 to 3.2]

6.1 Some terms

Population – a number of organisms of the same species that live in a given area.

Population size – the number of individuals in the group.

Carrying capacity – the maximum population size that can be supported indefinitely by a particular environment.

Limiting factors operate to check animal populations. These include:

1 food, water or oxygen supply;
2 availability of light;
3 predators and parasites of the species;
4 lack of shelter or availability of space;
5 diseases of the species;
6 accumulation of toxic waste;
7 climatic conditions; and
8 natural disasters, e.g. hurricanes, flooding, volcanic eruptions.

A population allowed to grow unchecked will produce a curve of growth as shown in Fig. 6.1. This is easily demonstrated by counting species that are small and can be grown in the laboratory, e.g. bacteria, yeast or small mammals (e.g. mice). As can be seen from the graph, such unchecked population growth would result in high numbers. In nature, however, natural checks stop the curve of growth rising continuously (i.e. toxic substances accumulate in bacterial colonies, alcohol accumulates in yeast colonies and food runs out in mouse colonies).

Fig. 6.2 shows an example of this in a colony of sheep introduced into the island of Tasmania in 1814.

Fig. 6.1 *A population of mice growing with no limiting factors*

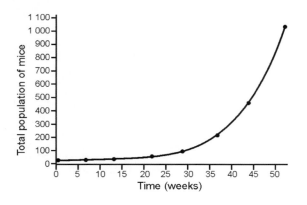

After 50 years, the growth curve of the population levelled out when the limiting factors of food and disease became effective.

Fig. 6.2 *Growth of population of sheep introduced into Tasmania – limiting factors begin to operate after 50 years*

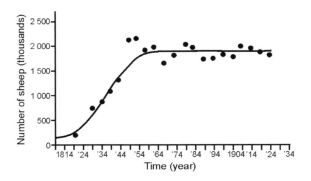

A similar example from America (see Fig. 6.3) shows the growth of a population of deer on a plateau after their predators (mountain lions, wolves and coyotes) had been removed. There was plenty of food for the deer and their numbers increased rapidly. The population eventually overshot the carrying capacity of the region and, due to lack of food and disease, the numbers crashed down. After a time, as the food supply improved, their numbers would again increase up to the carrying capacity of the region.

Fig. 6.3 *Population growth and crash of an isolated colony of deer on the Kaibab plateau, Arizona*

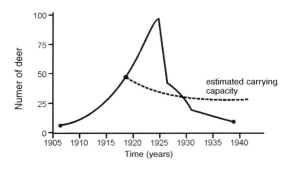

This type of **predator–prey relationship** is very important in a natural habitat and Fig. 6.4 shows an example of this with the lynx (a type of large cat) and the hare in North America. Notice that:

1 the rise in **number of the predators lags behind** that of the **prey**, i.e. the hares have to increase first before the lynx can take advantage of the increased food supply;

2 there are always **fewer predators than prey** (secondary consumers are always less numerous than primary consumers).

Fig. 6.4 *Prey-predator fluctuations of a lynx (broken line) and the hare (solid line)*

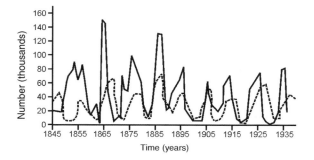

6.2 Human populations

Human populations are also subject to limiting factors, specifically:

1 shortage of food;
2 physical overcrowding;
3 disease, specifically those caused by pathogens; and
4 changing environmental conditions (which may actually be a direct result of human activities).

Their effects, however, have gradually become modified throughout the period of human existence, for the following reasons:

- Human societies have developed a division of labour whereby food producers (farmers) are separated from the rest of the community. This specialisation, as well as greatly increased efficiency, results in **large surpluses of food** in the developed nations of the world. Research continues to develop plant species that are high yielding even under adverse environmental conditions, such as drought.
- Humans have **few predators**; those that do exist (lions, tigers, crocodiles, wolves etc.) make little impact on population size.
- **Infectious and contagious diseases** have **not** been conquered. Cholera, malaria, AIDS and tuberculosis are a major source of concern. International travel makes the spread of these diseases easier. The abuse of antibiotics has resulted in the resistance of certain strains of bacteria to these drugs.

These factors do not have equal influence throughout the world – there is a difference between developed nations and the developing nations. So people in developed nations tend to have a greater life expectancy than others.

In theory all the people in the world could be fed from the present world production of food.

In theory birth control programmes could be developed to slow the rapid increase in population size.

Fertility

Richer, better-fed people tend to have smaller families, with a birth rate of about 25 per 1000 of the population. Poor, underfed people have higher birth rates of 55 per 100.

This is a contradictory statement since it has been shown by research that **better nutrition increases fertility**. The explanation probably lies in social rather than biological factors.

1 **Standard of living** – the higher the standard of living (among richer people), the smaller the family size. In less developed countries, where birth control may not be practised extensively, birth rates are higher in comparison to developed countries.
2 The **employment of women** and their social status in developed countries has meant a drop in the birth rate.
3 **Religious beliefs** also have an effect on the number of children produced by each female in a country.
4 In times of **economic depression**, birth rates fall; in boom times (when people are earning more money) birth rates tend to rise.

Human population growth and its influence on resources

Great population expansion has only taken place in the last few hundred years. This increase, together with the widespread growth of cities, has necessitated the production and distribution of food in enormous quantities. The problem lies, however, in its **unequal distribution**: some societies waste food while others starve.

The development of farming led to the **cutting down of forests** to provide land for agriculture. The result has been that deserts have replaced the forests. Slash-and-burn methods of cultivation have led to a reduction in soil fertility, soil erosion and flooding.

The desire for farming land, the need for wood for manufacturing purposes and the use of paper for newsprint all outstrip any replacement of forest by tree planting.

The discovery and use of oil and natural gas have provided more sources of energy. All of these **resources**, however, are limited and will probably **run out** in the next hundred years. Additionally, the burning of fossil fuels contributes to atmospheric pollution, depletion of the ozone layer and acid rain.

7 Pollution and conservation

[syllabus sections E4.1 to 4.2; E5.1 to 5.3]

7.1 Pollution

Pollution is the release, into the environment, of substances or heat energy that cause damage to the biotic and abiotic components of the environment. Human activity is usually the cause of pollution.

Air pollution

Air pollution, i.e. the release of harmful materials into the atmosphere, has been brought about mainly by industrialisation. Important atmospheric pollutants include chlorofluorocarbons (CFCs), sulphur dioxide, hydrocarbons and nitrogen oxides.

Smoke

Smoke results from the burning of carbon fuels (coal, coke and oil).

Sulphur dioxide

The burning of industrial fuels also releases sulphur dioxide. In combination with water this produces acids resulting in rainfall that corrodes metals and building stonework – acid rain.

Carbon monoxide

Internal combustion engines (cars and lorries) produce carbon monoxide. In large cities with congested traffic, 200 parts per million (ppm) have been measured; 1000 ppm is lethal to humans and as little as 100 ppm can cause nausea.

Carbon dioxide

The level of carbon dioxide in the air has been rising over recent years. It has been shown to be produced by the burning of fossil and aviation fuels. The additional carbon dioxide traps heat escaping from the earth and contributes to an exaggerated **greenhouse effect** – the warming of the Earth's atmosphere and the melting of the polar ice caps.

Dust

Vast quantities of grit and dust are poured into the air every year from bauxite mining activity, cement works, and power stations. Greater efforts must be made to develop cleansing processes for these industries.

Water pollution

Marine pollution

The sea surrounds the Caribbean islands and so the pollution of the marine environment is of great importance. Marine pollution leads to a reduction in the diversity of species in these areas.

Sewage

Many coastal cities discharge sewage into the sea in order to avoid the expense of building proper sewage works. The raw sewage is often pumped out through large pipes up to a mile out to sea. Although much of this material is broken down and makes its way through the food chains of the sea, dangerous pathogens can accumulate in the water. The action of wind and tide can sweep back the effluent into shallow water and onto the beaches. Shellfish can be contaminated by microorganisms and, when eaten, can cause intestinal disease. Every effort must be made by municipal authorities to build proper sewage-treatment plants. Pollution of marine environments leads to the death of fish and destruction of the coral reef habitats, beach erosion, loss of fish stocks and decreased aesthetic and recreational value.

Oil

Tankers carrying oil often illegally discharge oil into the sea while cleaning out their tanks. Millions of litres are released each year in this way, although it is strictly illegal. There have been numerous occasions on which oil tankers have been wrecked and have released their oil into the sea in large quantities. There have also been spillages from oil fields that extract oil from beneath the seabed.

Bacteria can break down oil in the sea, but in the short term, this oil is deadly to wildlife.

Fresh water pollution

Rivers have always been used by industry as a means of cheap disposal of waste products:

Sewage

Raw sewage is sometimes discharged into rivers. This often happens in large cities when the production of sewage exceeds the capacity of the sewage plants. The result is that the bacteria increase very rapidly and use up all the oxygen in the river, with the result that living organisms die. Improper sewage disposal results in offensive odours, leads to the bacterial contamination of drinking water, and the spread of disease, such as cholera.

Detergents

Modern washing powders, used to excess, pass into the sewage and are then flushed into rivers. The detergent remains active even in treated sewage. Some detergents contain phosphates, which pollute the water and cause an abnormal growth of algae. Some newer detergents are easily broken down by algae.

Industrial waste
Factories often discharge their waste chemicals, which may include metals such as lead, mercury, zinc and copper, into rivers. These metals are poisons and are very dangerous to fish and other freshwater life. The metals build up in food chains and can even reach humans.

Farming
Modern farming practices of concentrating livestock in large numbers on feedlots produces vast quantities of manure that is sometimes flushed into rivers. Chemical fertilisers that stimulate plant growth (nitrates and sulphates) are also washed by rain into ponds causing increased growth of aquatic plants.

Temperature changes
Water is used as a coolant for industrial purposes and in the cooling towers of power stations. The water is extracted from rivers and then returned to the river further downstream. This returning water is at a higher temperature than the river. Oxygen is less soluble in water at higher temperatures and therefore levels of this gas are reduced. Aquatic organisms cannot survive under these conditions.

Improper garbage disposal
This can lead to flooding, especially where garbage is disposed of in waterways. Medical garbage poses a hazard to human health. Uncontrolled fires at dumpsites can produce noxious fumes.

7.2 Conservation
Conservation is the practice of preventing species extinction and maintaining diversity of species in an ecosystem. It involves the careful management of resources and the preservation of natural habitats.

Our resources are limited
The world's resources of raw materials are not unlimited. They can be divided into:
1 **renewable resources** – these are capable of being replaced by natural ecological cycles or sound management practices (e.g. water, air, soil and forests);
2 **non-renewable resources** – these are usually taken from the earth by an extraction process; their amounts are fixed and therefore they will eventually run out and no longer be available (e.g. minerals, coal, oil and natural gas).

Renewable resources become non-renewable due to human abuse and pollution.

Recycling waste
To conserve these non-renewable materials much of our waste could be re-used. In many parts of the world, significant efforts are being made to recycle a number of manufactured products.

Plastics
Plastics can be recycled to make several types of plastic products. The recycling of plastics is complicated by the fact that there are several different types that must be separated for processing. Soda bottles can be recycled to make fibrefill used in sleeping bags, carpet fibres, rope and pillows. Polystyrene, found in disposable hot cups and packaging material, can be recycled into plastic lumber, cassette tape boxes and flowerpots.

Glass
Glass bottles are collected, separating clear from coloured glass. They are then returned for processing and can be melted down and recast. Recycled glass is cheaper than plastic.

Newspapers
Newspapers are collected and returned for pulping. This pulp can be used again for making cardboard boxes and packing paper. In this way the destruction of the forest can be slowed down a little.

Tin
Collection of many types of tin can permits us to extract the tin for resmelting.

Iron and steel
Many objects today are made of these metals, from washing machines to cars. When they end up in scrap metal yards, they provide a source for recycled iron and steel.

Recycling requires sorting and collection of manufactured products. All of these types of recycling have problems of collection. It is not easy to persuade the public that they can help society in this way. However, the money received from this collection can often be used to aid some charity or club. Public education campaigns are necessary to encourage households to separate their domestic waste into its constituent parts for recycling, not least the organic material for making garden compost.

Vast amounts of the earth's deposits have been mined in the past and are still being extracted at an alarming rate. Iron ore has been mined for centuries to make every conceivable object from bridges to bicycles. These objects eventually rust away, dispersing the iron oxide over the surface of the earth. The same extraction without replacement applies to aluminium, nitrates, clay and so on. The mined materials are all non-renewable resources; the larger human populations become, the greater will be the demand for these resources.

Finding alternative energy supplies

Burning fossil fuels leads to pollution and furthermore there are only limited supplies of fuel present in the world. Alternative sources of energy include:

1 **Nuclear power** – nuclear fission is able to produce energy under strictly controlled conditions but there is always the danger of radioactive leaks or accidents. The disposal of radioactive waste is difficult because of its long-term radioactivity.
2 **Solar panels** – these exploit the energy of the sun directly. Production for domestic and commercial use is increasing. They have great importance for tropical countries with plenty of sunlight.
3 **Wave power** – research is proceeding on small-scale models to produce energy using the power of waves in the sea.
4 **Wind power** – very large windmills can produce electric power from dynamos. There are of course problems in that the wind power can vary significantly within a short space of time.

Wiser ways of using land for food production

Air, water and soil are renewable resources that are vital for the food supply of the world's population. The modern farming practice of growing crops aided by artificial fertilisers tends to deplete the soil fertility and contribute to acidification of the soil. Humus gradually disappears and the soil no longer binds together, thus is much more likely to erode. There is a continual search for more land and more soil to be used to produce food. This is usually done in the following ways:

1 **Cutting down forests and jungles.** By cutting down forests and jungles, these ecosystems are lost forever. There is only a short-term use, however, because the exposed soil quickly loses its fertility. This practice should be discontinued, but it is difficult to explain this to land-hungry people.
2 **Using steep land.** On the lower slopes of mountains and hills, the land is normally covered with brush or scrub and is used for grazing. It can be brought into use for agriculture and made productive. Erosion by water is the main problem but this can be overcome by terracing – cultivating the land in strips. A wall of stones holds each strip back so that the soil is retained. A disadvantage is the fact that large-scale use of machinery is not possible.
3 **Irrigation.** Non-productive desert land can be brought into production by providing water. Israel and the USA have used this method with great success, but it does have its problems. Owing to rapid evaporation of water, salts build up in the top layer of soil so that the fertility gradually deteriorates.

Conservation of wildlife

As forests have been cut down, towns built and domestic grazing animals encroach on the open plains, the natural wildlife of the world becomes reduced. Many species have been made extinct and many are still threatened. Many organisations throughout the world have been formed to protect wildlife. What are the arguments in favour of their preservation?

1 Wild plants and animals form a **reservoir of breeding stock or genetic diversity** on which we may have to fall back in the future. Our present domestic plants and animals have all been developed from wild stock originally. If wild organisms are allowed to disappear, their breeding and genetic potential will be lost forever.
2 The dangers of using pesticides and herbicides can be avoided by adopting the **biological control** of pests, which is only possible if the wild is maintained.
3 The countryside in its unspoilt state must be maintained for the use of people. City dwellers need the open spaces for their **leisure time**. Many people enjoy the **study of wildlife**, e.g. bird-watching and photographing butterflies, moths, flowers and so on.

How can wildlife be preserved? What action can be taken?

1 Set up **National Parks** where animals and plants can be retained in their natural state.
2 Preserve **rare** animals in zoological parks or safari parks.
3 Encourage the development of **eco-tourism** in island states.
4 Stop the **trade in the furs and horns** of rare animals, e.g. leopard, cheetah, rhinoceros and elephant.
5 Ban the **taking of eggs** of sea turtles.
6 **Enforce closed seasons** for the shooting of birds, hunting of wildlife, harvesting of conch and lobsters.
7 Stop the **wholesale destruction of forests** for paper.
8 Stop **pollution damaging forests and lakes**.
9 **Renew and replant** areas where mining has damaged the landscape.

8 Cells and organisms

[syllabus sections B1.1 to 1.6]

8.1 Characteristics of living organisms

What do living organisms have in common? The following characteristics help us recognise living organisms:

1 **Cellular organisation** – organisms consist of one or more cells.
2 **Nutrition** – living things are active, requiring energy; for this they need food. Green plants make their own food by photosynthesis whereas animals eat other organisms (plants and animals).
3 **Respiration** – food obtained by synthesis or feeding is broken down to release energy. Generally this occurs in the presence of oxygen (*aerobic respiration*) but sometimes in the absence of oxygen (*anaerobic respiration*).
4 **Excretion** – all life processes result in the production of waste materials that must be eliminated.
5 **Sensitivity** – organisms respond to stimuli, i.e. changes inside or outside the organism. The environment within which organisms live is constantly changing, as is the internal environment of the organism. Being able to sense and adjust to changes enables life to continue within the habitat of each organism and within the organism so that all other life processes can proceed optimally.
6 **Homeostasis** – all living things maintain relatively constant internal conditions in spite of changes in their external environments.
7 **Heredity** – DNA – deoxyribonucleic acid is a molecule common to living organisms. This molecule provides the code for making proteins and so enzymes. Enzymes alter the rate at which molecules are broken down and formed in cells. DNA therefore controls all activity in living things. Dividing cells pass on their DNA to daughter cells formed.
8 **Reproduction** – living things are produced by others of their kind, by simple division (**asexual**) or by the fusion of gametes or sex cells (**sexual**).
9 **Growth** – food synthesised or obtained from the environment of the organism by feeding is used for conversion into new living material (**protoplasm**). Cells divide and enlarge; ultimately the organism grows to full size (**maturity**).
10 **Movement** – all organisms show movement but animals in particular are different from plants in their movement from place to place (**locomotion**). Animals need to move to find food and for a mate.

8.2 Differences between plants and animals

Fig. 8.1 *(a) Generalised animal cell*
(b) Plant cell

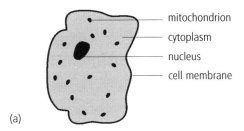

(a)

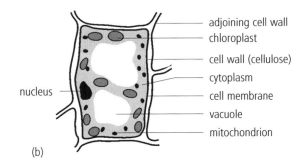

(b)

Table 8.1 *Differences between plants and animals*

Characteristic	Plants	Animals
Nutrition	Synthesise own food from inorganic substances (autotrophic)	Depend on ready-made food (heterotrophic)
Respiration	Little activity – little energy required	Very active – considerable energy required
Excretion	No excretion of nitrogenous waste	Excretion of nitrogenous waste
Response	Slow – by growth; activated by chemical substances	Fast – by movement; activated by chemical and nervous activity
Reproduction	Asexual and sexual	Mainly sexual
Growth	Slow – some have continuous growth	Slow – to a maximum size

Table 8.2 *Comparing plant and animal cells*

Green plants	Animals
Differences:	
Chlorophyll in chloroplasts	No chloroplast
Cell wall – consisting of cellulose	No cell wall
Large vacuoles	Vacuoles often absent or very small
Storage granules – starch grains in chloroplasts and cytoplasm; oil or lipid droplets, oils	Storage – glycogen and oil or lipid droplets and protein
Similarities:	
Cell surface membrane	
Mitochondria	
Nucleus containing chromosomes consisting of DNA and protein	

8.3 Cell theory

The basic unit of structure and function in living organisms is the cell; all cells arise from pre-existing cells. This concept is called the **cell theory**. The cell is a self-regulating chemical system; maintaining internal stability (homeostasis) is essential to its proper functioning. The boundary between the cell and its surroundings is the **plasma membrane** or **cell surface membrane**. The cell contains **cytoplasm**. Suspended in this cytoplasm are minute structures called **organelles**. These include the **nucleus**, **vacuoles**, **mitochondria**, and (in plant cells) **chloroplasts**. Cells contain DNA, which directs the growth and development of the cell. The DNA of bacterial cells is not confined to a nucleus, but the DNA of plant and animal cells is.

Cells are small and have a small surface area relative to their volume. The smaller the cell, the larger the surface-area to volume ratio, the more efficiently the cell can function.

8.4 Levels of organisation

Living organisms show increasing complexity of structure. Living organisms are made up of organic compounds based on the carbon molecule. The elements carbon, hydrogen, oxygen and nitrogen are most commonly present, forming molecules of carbohydrates, fats and proteins.

Molecules make up cells. Cells are specialised, carrying out one task, while other cells carry out other tasks. In multicellular organisms, specialised cells are organised into tissues. Tissues are groups of similar cells, along with intercellular fluid, which perform precise

Table 8.3 *Cell components and functions*

Component	Function
Cell wall	Protects and supports cell, maintains shape
Cytoplasm	Semi-fluid or aqueous, contains sugars, amino acids and proteins used by cell to carry out everyday activities
Cell membrane	Regulates that which enters and leaves the cell
Nucleus	Contains chromosomes consisting of DNA and protein; directs protein synthesis and cell division
Mitochondria	Site of respiration – produce energy for cell activities
Chloroplast	Site of photosynthesis – process by which plants make organic molecules
Vacuole	In plants – temporary store of sugars and amino acids, wastes and enzymes. Supports cell by osmotic uptake of water and so plant.

Table 8.4 *Levels of organisation*

Organism	Organelle	Cell	Tissue	Organ	System	Function
Plant	Chloroplast	Palisade	Mesophyll	Leaf	Photosynthetic	Makes organic molecules
	None	Xylem vessel	Vascular	Root, stem, leaf	Vascular	Transports water and mineral salts
Animal	Nucleus	White blood cell	Blood	Throughout blood vessels and heart	Circulatory/ vascular	Destroys invading micro-organisms
	Nucleus	Sensory neurone	Nervous	Brain or spinal cord	Nervous	Conducts impulses from sense organs

functions. Organs are made up of a number of different tissues and several organs together form an organ system. These levels of organisation allow for greater efficiency of the organism.

Molecules ——→ Organelles ——→ Cells ——→ Tissues ——→ Organs ——→ Organ systems ——→ Organisms (see Table 8.4, on p. 20)

8.5 Diffusion and osmosis

Substances required by the cell and those produced by the cell can cross the cell membrane by the processes of diffusion and osmosis.

Diffusion – the movement of a substance (ions or molecules of a dissolved solute or gas) that are in constant random motion, from a region of high concentration to a region of lower concentration. The process will continue until the concentration becomes uniform. Examples in living organisms include:
1. the diffusion of oxygen in air within the lung alveoli (air sacs) through the alveolar wall to blood capillaries surrounding the alveoli;
2. the diffusion of carbon dioxide in the opposite direction; and
3. the diffusion of air with a high concentration of carbon dioxide through the air spaces and cells of a leaf for photosynthesis.

Osmosis – this is the movement of water molecules across a partially permeable membrane (cell surface membrane, membrane surrounding vacuole) from a less concentrated solution to a more concentrated solution. The cytoplasm of a cell contains ions and molecules (sugars and amino acids) dissolved in water and is therefore an aqueous solution. The vacuole of plant cells contains a solution of sugars, amino acids, inorganic salts and waste products. Examples in living organisms include:
1. the passage of water from soil into root hairs;
2. the movement of water from the xylem of the leaf into the palisade and spongy mesophyll of the leaf; and
3. the passage of water from pond water into the cytoplasm of an *Amoeba*.

8.6 Concentration and the cell membrane

If two solutions have equal concentrations they are described as **isotonic**. If two solutions have unequal concentrations, we call the solution with the higher concentration (a concentrated solution with more solute than solvent) **hypertonic**, and that with the lower concentration (a dilute solution, with more solvent than solute) **hypotonic**. Water will move across a partially permeable membrane from a dilute solution to a concentrated solution.

In cells the cell membrane separates two aqueous solutions, one inside the cell (the cytoplasm) and one outside (the extracellular fluid). The direction of movement of water molecules across the membrane is determined by the concentration of each of the solutions.

8.7 Concentration, osmosis and the cell

Plant cells in a dilute solution take in water by osmosis. The cell swells due to the increased volume of the cytoplasm and vacuole. This exerts pressure on the cell membrane and cell wall. The cell is described as **turgid** (see Fig. 8.2 (a)). In herbaceous plants (with no secondary thickening) turgor pressure maintains the shape of the cells and the turgidity of the tissue gives mechanical support to the plant.

Plant cells in a concentrated solution lose water by osmosis. Initially the fall in the volume of the cell cytoplasm and vacuole lead to a fall in pressure within the cell, which is described as **flaccid** (see Fig. 8.2 (b)).

As the cell loses more water and the volume of the contents decreases even further, the cell membrane pulls away from the cell wall and the cell is **plasmolysed**. Plants wilt when cells are plasmolysed.

Animal cells placed in a dilute solution swell and eventually burst. The cell membrane is unable to withstand the increased pressure due to the increased volume of the cell contents.

Fig. 8.2 *(a) A plant cell in a dilute (hypotonic) solution is turgid (b) A plant cell in a concentrated (hypertonic) solution cell is flaccid*

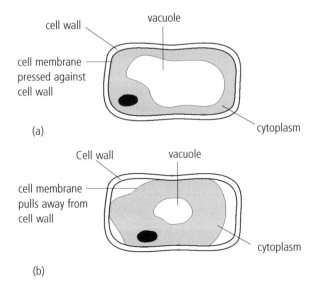

21

9 Metabolic reactions in the organism

[syllabus sections B2.7 to 2.8]

9.1 Anabolism and catabolism

We refer to all the biochemical reactions taking place in living organisms as **metabolism**. Biochemical reactions that make organic molecules are **anabolic reactions** and those that break down organic molecules are **catabolic reactions**.

Anabolic reaction involving the synthesis of a polypeptide (protein):

amino acids $\xrightarrow{\text{enzyme}}$ polypeptide + water

Catabolic reaction involving the breakdown of starch:

starch + water $\xrightarrow{\text{enzyme}}$ maltose

9.2 Metabolism requires enzymes

All metabolic reactions require **enzymes** in order to proceed efficiently. Enzymes are protein molecules produced by living cells, which act as biological catalysts. Very small quantities can speed up the rate of biochemical reactions. Enzymes may work outside of cells (as in the gut), or within cells during biological processes, (e.g. during photosynthesis and respiration). Some are bound to cell membranes, (e.g. digestive enzymes in the small intestine of humans). The cells of organisms contain many different enzymes.

The substance that the enzyme acts on is called the **substrate**. Enzymes work on the substrate and their action produces an **end-product**.

The mode of action of an enzyme is summarised below:

enzyme + substrate $\longrightarrow$ enzyme/substrate complex $\longrightarrow$ enzyme + product

9.3 Characteristics of enzymes

1. Catalyse one specific reaction.
2. Can bring about a reverse reaction.
3. Work fastest at the optimum temperature (37°C – 40°C for human enzymes).
4. Work fastest at the optimum pH (could be acid or alkaline conditions depending on the enzyme).
5. Can be destroyed (denatured) by heat (e.g. boiling).
6. Can be inactivated at extremely low temperatures (close to freezing point).
7. Can stop working in the presence of certain chemicals (cell poisons such as cyanide).

9.4 The effect of temperature on enzyme activity

Raising the temperature of an enzyme-catalysed reaction increases the rate of the reaction up to the **optimum temperature** for the enzyme. The optimum temperature (specifically temperature range) for an enzyme is that at which there is maximum activity of the enzyme. Heating provides both enzyme and substrate molecules with kinetic energy and so increases the frequency with which the molecules bump into or collide with each other.

Temperatures above the optimum (maximum activity) **denature** the enzyme – the bonds that maintain the shape of the molecule are disrupted; the enzyme loses its shape and cannot perform the catalytic function. Temperatures close to freezing point slow down the molecules, which with inadequate kinetic energy, become **inactivated**. Increasing the temperature to the optimum will activate them. The optimal temperature for enzymes of bacteria living in hot springs can be 70°C or higher.

9.5 The effect of pH on enzyme activity

The bonds maintaining the shape of the molecule are sensitive to pH. The optimum pH for an enzyme is that at which there is maximum activity of the enzyme.

The enzyme pepsin that digests proteins in the human stomach works best at pH 2.

Salivary amylase, which digests starch to maltose, works best at pH 6.5–7.5.

Pancreatic lipase that digests fats and oils (lipids) to fatty acids and glycerol works best at pH 7.00.

Catalase, which breaks down hydrogen peroxide, a by-product of cell metabolism, works best at pH 7.60.

Fig. 9.1 *(a) The effect of temperature on the activity of an enzyme (b) The activity of an enzyme related to pH*

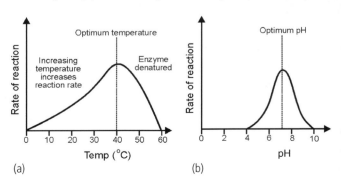

(a)

(b)

10 Reproduction in plants

[syllabus sections B9.6 to 9.11]

The flower is basically a modified stem bearing modified leaves (floral parts) arranged in circles (whorls) that arise at one level. The **pedicel** is the flower stalk, the stem that supports the flower or group of flowers (**inflorescence**). The **receptacle** is the upper end of the flower stalk (its shape can be concave or convex) – from it arise the floral parts.

10.1 Floral parts

1   An outermost ring of **sepals** forming the **calyx**, usually green in colour. These enclose and protect the flower when they are at the bud stage.
2   **Petals** forming the **corolla** lie within the calyx and surround the stamens and carpels – coloured and conspicuous in insect-pollinated flowers, but small or absent in wind-pollinated flowers. The lower part of petals may be joined to form a tube. The calyx and corolla together are termed the **perianth**.
3   Stamens form the **androecium** or male parts. Each stamen consists of a stalk or **filament** and two joined lobes called the **anthers**. Inside the anthers are pollen sacs that split when ripe to release pollen. The minute grains of pollen contain male gametes.
4   **Carpels** form the **gynaecium** or female parts. There may be several carpels present in a flower and they are usually joined to form a single

structure (**pistil**). This consists of the **ovary** (a hollow structure containing one or more ovules) and a **style** bearing a **stigma** (see Fig. 10.1). Pollen grains stick to the stigma when pollination occurs. Each ovule contains a female nucleus.

10.2 Pollination

Pollination is the transfer of pollen from the anther to the stigma in a flowering plant. In **self-pollination** pollen is transferred from the stamen to the stigma of the same flower or to another flower of the same plant. In **cross-pollination** pollen is transferred from the stamen of one flower to a stigma of another flower on another plant of the same species.

Wind pollination

Flowers of wind-pollinated plants are usually inconspicuous with large stamens, long filaments and feathery stigmas. Pollen grains are dry, small and smooth so they are easily blown by the wind. All grasses use this method of pollen transfer.

Insect pollination

Flowers of insect-pollinated plants may have conspicuous, coloured petals and are often constructed

Fig. 10.1 *Floral parts of a typical open flower*

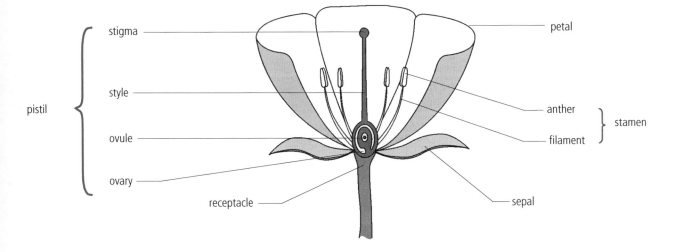

Fig. 10.2 *Half flower of the Barbados Pride (Caesalpinia pulcherrima)*

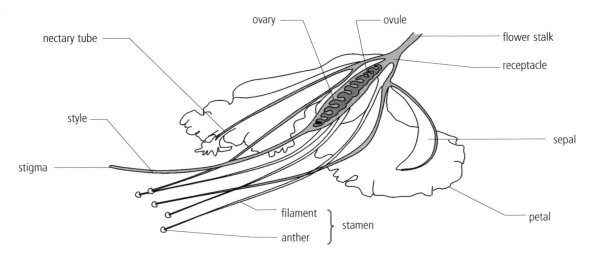

to permit an insect visitor of one particular type (e.g. bees or butterflies). Insects are attracted to these flowers by food (pollen and/or nectar) and are drawn by the scent of the flower. Insects are often guided to the food by markings on the petals called nectar guides. The pollen is sticky and rough so that it attaches easily to the insect visitor. Flowers may be open (Kingston buttercup) or tubular (Periwinkle). If the corolla is not prominent, insects may be attracted by coloured bracts e.g. *Bougainvillea* and *Poinsettia*.

Fig. 10.3 *Diagram showing parts of a spikelet of a grass*

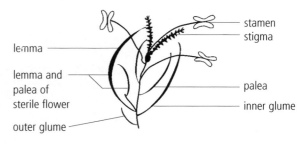

Fig. 10.4 *A portion of an inflorescence (with flowers at different stages of development) of Guinea grass (Panicum maximum)*

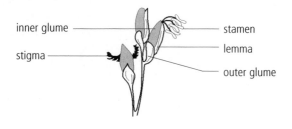

Bird pollination

Humming birds and honeysuckers visit flowers for nectar and collect pollen on their breast feathers e.g. the Barbados Pride (*Caesalpinia pulcherrima*).

10.3 Fertilisation

When the pollen grain reaches the stigma it produces a **pollen tube** that grows through the stigma and down the style. It continues through the ovary wall and enters the **ovule** by way of the **micropyle**. The tip of the pollen tube releases two male nuclei, one of which fuses with the nucleus of the ovule (fertilisation). The other fuses with nuclei of the embryo sac. The ovule becomes the **seed** with the embryo plant enclosed within the **testa**.

After fertilisation the floral parts are shed and the **ovary** develops into the **fruit**. The fruit consists of those parts of the flower that persist after fertilisation. The following changes occur:

1 The ovule becomes the seed that contains the embryo and (sometimes) the endosperm – covered by the testa; the micropyle remains.
2 The ovary wall becomes the fruit wall or **pericarp**.
3 Parts that sometimes persist:
   (a) the receptacle – in pome (e.g. apple)
   (b) the style – in achene of Clematis
   (c) the sepals – in berry (e.g. tomato).

When released, the **fruit** has two scars, that of its attachment to the pedicel and to the style. The **seed** has only one scar (**hilum**) where it was attached to the ovule stalk (**funicle**).

24

Fig. 10.5 *Seed of the red pea (Phaseolus vulgaris) (a) seed (b) testa removed (c) testa removed, cotyledons separated*

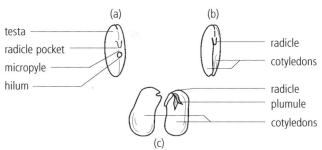

10.4 Seed

The seed (Fig. 10.6) contains the plant embryo consisting of young shoot (**plumule**), young root (**radicle**) and the seed leaves (**cotyledons**). In **dicotyledons** (dicots) there are two cotyledons. Some seeds have food reserves in a special tissue called the **endosperm**. Seeds may be endospermic (e.g. castor oil) or non-endospermic (e.g. red pea).

Germination

This is the process by which the seed of a flowering plant starts to develop into a seedling.

Conditions required for germination

All the conditions listed below are essential for a high rate of respiration releasing energy for growth.

1 **Minimum temperature** – germination will not commence until the soil is warm enough. Thus, in countries with a cold winter climate, germination begins when the soil begins to warm up in the spring.
2 **Water** – needed to activate enzymes and aid hydrolysis of food reserves into soluble, transportable materials.
3 **Oxygen** – present in soil air and available to be taken up by seeds to allow aerobic respiration.

When seeds germinate, water is absorbed and enzymes convert insoluble food reserves (starch or oil) into soluble compounds. These are transported to the growing points of the **radicle** (young root) and **plumule** (young shoot). This results in an initial loss of mass until the young leaves begin to photosynthesise. The radicle penetrates the soil, producing root hairs to increase the uptake of water and dissolved salts. Lateral roots develop, improving anchorage in the soil. The plumule pushes up through the soil, straightening as it produces the first leaves.

Types of germination

1 **Hypogeal** – the seed containing the **cotyledons** remains below the soil. The plumule grows upwards due to lengthening of the **epicotyl** (see Fig. 10.6 (a)).
2 **Epigeal** – the seed containing the **cotyledons** is pushed upwards above the soil by the rapid growth of the **hypocotyl** (see Fig. 10.6 (b)).

Seedlings and mature plants grow by cell division in regions of the plant called **meristems**. These are principally at the tips of root and shoot and are called **apical meristems** or growing points.

Fig. 10.6 *(a) Epigeal germination – red pea (Phaseolus vulgaris) (b) Hypogeal germination – Gungo pea (Cajanus cajun)*

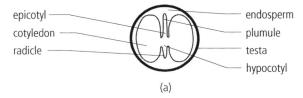

(a)

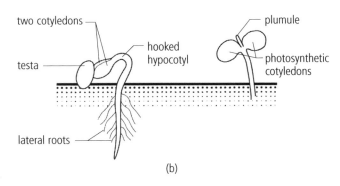

(b)

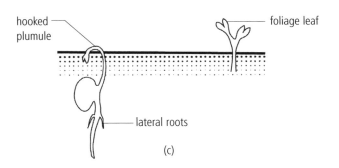

(c)

The cells are constantly dividing by **mitosis**. Further back from the tip of the root or stem cells **vacuoles** develop and enlarge. They eventually differentiate into tissues such as parenchyma, sclerenchyma, xylem and phloem. Three zones can therefore be recognised at root and shoot tip:

1 zone of cell division
2 zone of cell expansion
3 zone of cell differentiation.

10.5 Dispersal of fruits and seeds

Dispersal by wind

1 Minute seeds of orchids blown as dust.
2 Winged fruits and seeds – pericarp or testa extended to form a wing or wings, e.g.
  (a) fruit – Crow
  (b) seed – Torch wood (*Techoma*) and Whitewood.
3 Plumed (feathery) fruits and seeds – tufts of hairs act as parachutes, e.g.
  (a) fruit – Clematis
  (b) seed – French cotton (*Calotropis*) and Silk cotton (*Ceiba*)

Dispersal by animals

Hooked fruits – Different parts of the flower develop hooks that can be caught up on the fur of animals (or human clothing), e.g. Bidens – hooked persistent calyx (see Fig. 10.7), sweethearts (*Desmodium*) – hooked hairs on the pericarp.

Fig. 10.7 *Achene of Bidens – animal dispersal*

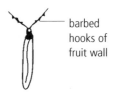

barbed hooks of fruit wall

Edible fruits – Berries and drupes are succulent fruits attractive to animals. These can be eaten and the seeds swallowed. They later appear in dung where they germinate. Animals may discard seeds that are hard after they have eaten the fruit. The pome is also edible but the succulent part is the swollen receptacle (see Figures 10.8 and 10.9), e.g. guava, tomato, mango, hog plum, apple.

Fig. 10.8 *(a) Legume of Caesalpinia – split pod (b) Berry of tomato (Lycopersicon esculentum) – animal dispersal*

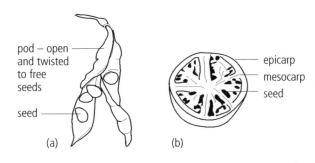

pod – open and twisted to free seeds

seed

epicarp
mesocarp
seed

(a)   (b)

Fig. 10.9 *Drupe of mango (Mangifera) vertical section – animal dispersal*

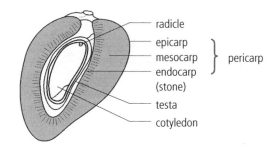

radicle
epicarp
mesocarp } pericarp
endocarp (stone)
testa
cotyledon

Dispersal by explosive fruits

Fruits burst and throw out the seeds, e.g. Geranium (see Figures 10.7, 10.8, 10.10).

Fig. 10.10 *(a) Geranium – explosive mechanism (b) Clematis – wind dispersal (c) Capsule of Balsam (Impatiens) – explosive mechanism*

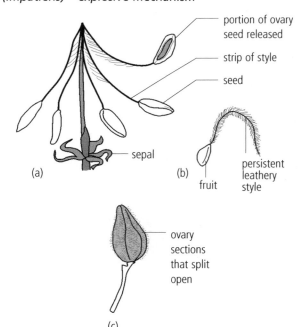

portion of ovary seed released
strip of style
seed

sepal

(a)   (b)

persistent leathery style
fruit

ovary sections that split open

(c)

Dispersal by water

Many plants grow near rivers and seashores, and their fruits and seeds, after falling in the water, can be carried considerable distances, e.g. coconut (see Fig. 10.11).

Fig. 10.11 *Vertical section of a coconut, a drupe – water dispersal*

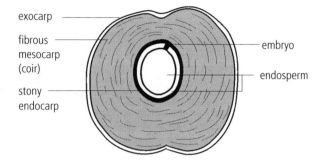

exocarp

fibrous mesocarp (coir)

stony endocarp

embryo

endosperm

Dispersal by humans

By their actions, humans have dispersed many plants around the world:

1 **Trade** – the movement of wool, timber, and cereals have all contributed to the transfer of species from one country to another.
2 **Botanists** have collected plants from all corners of the earth during the last 500 years. These have been replanted in botanic and private gardens far from their place of origin.
3 **Amateur gardeners** and horticulturalists collect plants on their travels and bring them back to their own country, often without consideration of the possible results such as the transfer of pests and diseases.
4 **Clothes** transport plant fruits and seeds short and even long distances when we walk through grassy fields.

11 Photosynthesis

Photosynthesis – an autotrophic form of nutrition in green plants. The pigment chlorophyll absorbs light energy and uses it to produce carbohydrates, releasing oxygen as a waste product.

11.1 Leaf structure

The leaf is well designed to carry out several functions. It is supported by a central midrib (main vein) running through the lamina or leaf blade. The petiole attaches the leaf to the stem. Running through the petiole into the midrib is a vein formed of xylem and phloem. The xylem carries water and salts to the leaf while the phloem carries sugars and amino acids away from the leaf. See Figs. 11.1 and 11.2 that show the internal and surface structure of the leaf.

The epidermal cells normally have no chloroplasts. Guard cells are unusual epidermal cells in that they do have chloroplasts. The upper layer of cells, within the leaf, consists of palisade cells each with numerous chloroplasts. Below the palisade mesophyll layer is the spongy mesophyll, which has fewer chloroplasts and air spaces between the cells. The lower epidermis has pores (stomata) opening to the air spaces. Each stoma is surrounded by two guard cells. The epidermal cells are irregular in shape and fit closely into each other, rather like stones in a pavement.

11.2 Adaptation of the leaf for photosynthesis

1 Large surface area for absorption of light and exchange of O_2 and CO_2.
2 Leaf at right angles to light for maximum absorption.
3 Chloroplasts packed in the upper (palisade) layer.
4 Chlorophyll of chloroplasts absorbs red and blue light.
5 Maximum leaf surface due to arrangement of leaves not overlapping.

The process of photosynthesis is represented in a simplified form as follows using a word equation and chemical notation: (see p. 29)

Fig. 11.1 *Vertical section through a leaf*

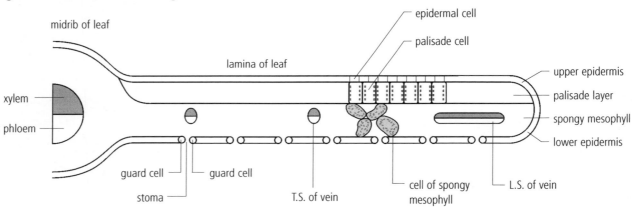

Fig. 11.2 *Guard cells and a stoma (a) stoma closed (b) stoma open*

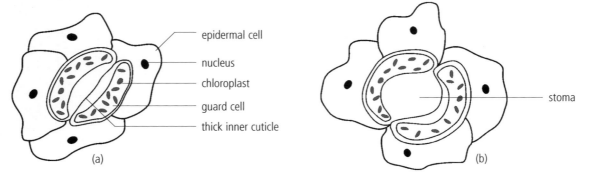

$$\text{carbon dioxide + water} \xrightarrow[\text{enzymes}]{\text{light energy absorbed by cholophyll}}$$

carbohydrate (glucose) + oxygen

$$6CO_2 + 6H_2O \xrightarrow[\text{enzymes}]{\text{light energy absorbed by cholophyll}} C_6H_{12}O_6 + 6O_2$$

Carbon dioxide – in air enters the leaf pores or stomata and passes through the air spaces of the leaf by diffusion. It dissolves in water on the cell surfaces and diffuses into the cells to the chloroplasts.
Water – absorbed by the root hairs of the root. Enters the root hairs by osmosis.
Light – red and blue wavelengths of light are most important in photosynthesis (green light is reflected or passes through the leaf completely). Light energy is used to split water molecules, releasing O_2 and producing energy as ATP and H^+. CO_2 is converted to carbohydrates using ATP and H^+.

11.3 How products of photosynthesis are used

1 **Synthesis**

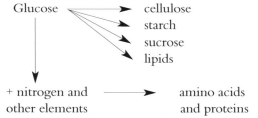

2 **Respiration** – glucose is used to provide energy in cell respiration. It is extremely reactive and so is converted quickly to sucrose.

2 **Storage** – sucrose, starch, lipids and amino acids are transported to storage organs, e.g. sugar cane stems store sucrose; coconut fruits store lipids; potatoes, cereal seeds (corns and legumes) store starch (see Table 11.1).
3 **Growth** – cellulose is a component of cell walls and is used in the formation of new cells and the enlargement of existing cells.
4 **Regulation** – stored amino acids can be used to synthesise regulating proteins: enzymes and growth regulators (auxins).

11.4 Minerals in plant metabolism

Three basic elements: carbon, hydrogen, oxygen are incorporated into the plant by the process of photosynthesis. The remainder must come from the soil where the elements are present as salts or ions. Table 11.1 shows an analysis of a corn plant in which elements are expressed as a percentage of dry weight:

Table 11.1 *Analysis of a corn plant*

Basic elements	% D.W.	Major elements	of D.W.
Carbon	43.5	Nitrogen	1.5
Oxygen	44.4	Sulphur	0.2
Hydrogen	6.2	Phosphorus	0.2
		Calcium	0.2
		Iron	0.1
		Magnesium	0.2
		Potassium	0.9
Total	**94.1%**		**3.3%**

The remaining 2.6% are minor elements.
Major elements are needed by the plant cells for:
1 synthesis of proteins;
2 cell formation;
3 suitable aqueous solutions for enzyme activity.

Table 11.2 *Elements and their role in plant metabolism*

Element	Role in the plant	Signs of deficiency	Inorganic fertiliser
Nitrogen	Amino acid, thus healthy growth	Yellow leaves, thus stunted growth	Sodium nitrate and ammonium sulphate
Potassium	Amino acid and thus protein synthesis, cell in cell division	Yellow leaves, poor growth and early death	Potassium sulphate and potassium chloride
Phosphorus	Promotes root growth, protein synthesis, synthesis of ATP and nucleic acids (DNA)	Poor root growth	Calcium phosphate
Sulphur	Synthesis of proteins	Yellow leaves	Potassium sulphate
Iron	Chlorophyll synthesis	Yellow leaves	Complete fertilisers
Calcium	Cell wall (middle lamella) calcium phosphate formation at root and stem apices	Poor root growth, stunted growth	Lime (calcium hydroxide)
Magnesium	Formation of cholorophyll	Yellow leaves, stunted growth	Magnesium sulphate

Table 11.3 *Standard tests for biochemicals*

Biochemical	Test	Observation
Starch	Add 1 to 2 drops of dilute iodine solution (iodine in potassium iodide) to a starch suspension.	Brown coloured iodine changes to blue-black colour.
Reducing sugar (glucose, maltose)	Mix equal quantities of Benedict's solution and a glucose solution. Boil or heat in a water bath.	Blue colour changes to a range of colours according to the concentration of the glucose solution (green, yellow, orange, red or brown precipitate).
Non-reducing sugar (sucrose)	Add 3 drops of dilute hydrochloric acid to the sucrose solution. Boil in a water bath for 2–3 minutes. Cool and add sodium hydrogencarbonate until fizzing stops. Repeat Benedict's solution tests. (Boiling with acid hydrolyses the sucrose to reducing sugar which will now react with the test reagents.)	Blue colour changes to colours stated above.
Protein	Add 1 cm^3 of sodium or potassium hydroxide solution to 2 cm^3 of egg albumen. Add 1% copper sulphur solution drop by drop.	Violet, mauve or light purple colour appears.
Fat or oil	(i) Rub on to a piece of paper.	A spot transmitting light appears on the paper. (This should be compared to a water spot which dries, whereas the fat spot does not.)
	(ii) Pour 2 cm^3 of ethanol into test tube and add a small volume of oil (palm oil or olive oil). Shake and then pour the mixture into a second test tube containing about 2 cm^3 of water.	Milky emulsion is formed.

12 Human nutrition

Heterotrophs gain the nutrients they require from the complex organic molecules they consume. Humans are heterotrophs that feed holozoically; they have a digestive tract (alimentary canal) and so ingest, digest, absorb and assimilate organic matter. Undigested material is eliminated or egested.

Ingestion – the intake of organic food into the body.
Digestion – the breakdown of large insoluble molecules of food into small, soluble, diffusible molecules. Digestion can be (a) **mechanical** – breakdown of food by teeth and by gut muscles (mastication or chewing and peristalsis) or (b) **chemical** – breakdown (hydrolysis) of food by digestive enzyme action.
Absorption – the process whereby soluble molecules enter living cells.
Assimilation – the process whereby simple molecules are used by the body, e.g. amino acids formed into proteins (in cytoplasm, as enzymes) and glucose used for cell respiration to provide energy.
Egestion – the process whereby undigested food is eliminated from the body, i.e. defecation.

Food taken in through the mouth enters the buccal cavity where teeth cut or chew food. Mastication is the breakdown of food by teeth as it is moved around by the tongue and moistened by saliva. There are four types of teeth: **incisors** for biting; **canines** for tearing and chewing; **premolars and molars** (cheek teeth) for chewing.

Incisors, canines and premolars first grow as a set of 'milk teeth' that are replaced during childhood by a permanent set. Molars are added to the milk set to complete the permanent set.

Humans are **omnivorous;** they have biting incisors and small canines. Human premolars and molars have rounded cusps for chewing. Humans eat a mixed diet of meat and plant material.

12.1 The human alimentary canal

Specialised regions and functions

Buccal cavity Food ingested. Masticated by teeth, moistened by saliva. Digestion begins.

$$\text{Starch} \xrightarrow{\text{salivary amylase}} \text{maltose}$$

Chewed food is rolled into a bolus by the tongue. Saliva binds food particles into a bolus, which is swallowed.

Oesophagus The bolus is moved by peristalsis (wave-like contractions of circular muscle) from the buccal cavity to the stomach.

Stomach Contraction of muscular walls mixes food. Gastric juice is released. It is composed of:

1. hydrochloric acid – provides acid medium for action of pepsin, kills many bacteria (amylase is ineffective here because pH is not optimal for it);
2. pepsin – hydrolyses proteins to polypeptides (i.e. splits large molecules with addition of water molecules to smaller molecules);

Fig. 12.1 *Sections through (a) incisor and (b) molar teeth*

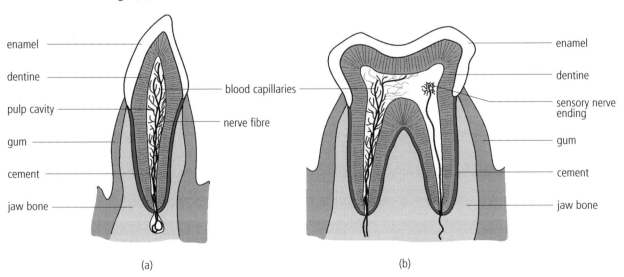

(a)   (b)

Fig. 12.2 *The human alimentary canal*

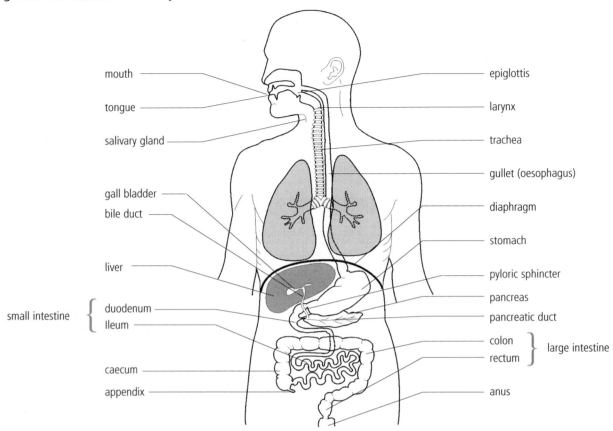

3 rennin – found in young children, converts soluble milk protein – caseinogen – into insoluble casein, which can then be acted upon by pepsin.

The stomach wall is not digested by its own secretions because a layer of mucus protects it. Aspirin and alcohol are absorbed directly across the stomach wall. Food is formed into **chyme** and exits through the pyloric sphincter (a ring of muscle).

Duodenum. First part of small intestine where food is digested. It receives:
1 **Bile** – from the gall bladder of the liver via the bile duct; this bile neutralises stomach acid; it contains bile salts that emulsify fats (fats to droplets). It is not an enzyme.
2 **Pancreatic juice** – from the pancreas via the pancreatic duct; three main enzymes in this secretion act as follows:

$$\text{proteins} \xrightarrow{\text{trypsin}} \text{peptides + amino acids;}$$

$$\text{fats (lipids)} \xrightarrow{\text{lipase}} \text{fatty acids + glycerol;}$$

$$\text{starch} \xrightarrow{\text{amylase}} \text{maltose.}$$

Ileum. This is the largest part of the small intestine. Intestinal juice is secreted here that contains water and mucus to increase the volume of fluid in the gut. Enzymes in this region are bound to the cell surface membrane of the microvilli.

$$\text{sucrose} \xrightarrow{\text{sucrase}} \text{glucose + fructose}$$

$$\text{maltose} \xrightarrow{\text{maltase}} \text{glucose}$$

$$\text{peptides} \xrightarrow{\text{erepsin}} \text{amino acids}$$

$$\text{fats} \xrightarrow{\text{lipase}} \text{fatty acids + glycerol}$$

Colon. Absorbs water from the faeces (undigested food, dead cells and bacteria).

Rectum. Faeces passed out by egestion. Absorption of the end products of digestion occurs through the gut wall of the duodenum and ileum aided by the large surface area available. The walls are folded to form villi, which contain microvilli on their surfaces.

1 Monosaccharides and amino acids diffuse into the blood capillaries of the villi, which converge to form the hepatic portal vein that delivers the absorbed molecules to the liver.

2 Fatty acids and glycerol enter the cells of the villi. They are reconverted to fat that enters the lacteal (core) of the villi and pass into the blood stream via the lymphatic system (see Transport).

3 Mineral salts, vitamins and water are also absorbed in the small intestine.

4 Some of the glucose transported to the liver is distributed around the body where it is used for respiration. Excess glucose is converted to glycogen and fat, which can be stored in the liver.

5 Amino acids are used to make new cell materials, repair damaged tissue, and form enzymes and hormones. Surplus amino acids cannot be stored and are converted into urea that travels in the bloodstream to the kidneys, from which they are excreted in the urine. The remainder of the amino acid molecule is converted to glycogen and stored.

6 Absorbed fats bypass the liver and enter the bloodstream via a lymphatic duct in the neck. Fats represent the major energy store in the body and are stored below the skin in adipose tissue, and around the heart and kidneys.

12.2 Controlling blood sugar

Normally, homeostatic mechanisms ensure that blood sugar remains level in the body as we see in Fig. 12.3.

Diabetes mellitus can occur when this homeostatic mechanism breaks down. Diabetes mellitus is a

Fig. 12.3 *Homeostatic control of blood sugar levels*

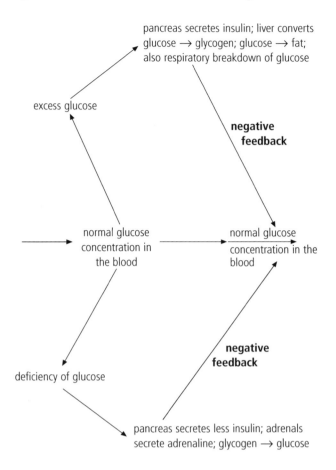

physiological disorder in which the concentration of blood glucose cannot be properly regulated either because the pancreas does not produce enough insulin or because the cells do not take up glucose in response to insulin. Regulating the carbohydrate intake, regular exercise, maintaining a healthy weight and controlling blood sugar levels are necessary to ensure that all the glucose in the blood stream can be used by the body.

13 The human diet

13.1 Dietary terms

Diet – all the food and drink we consume that supply nutrients to the body.

Balanced diet – is one that contains correct proportions and amounts of the various nutrients, water and dietary fibre for the age and activity of the individual, thus maintaining a healthy body.

Malnutrition – under-nutrition and over-nutrition constitute malnutrition.

Vegetarianism – vegetarians do not consume meat often due to religious and health choices.

Lacto–ovo vegetarians consume milk and milk products (cheese and butter), eggs and plant material.

Lacto vegetarians consume milk, milk products and plant material.

Vegans consume plant material only and must carefully plan their diets, which may be lacking in essential amino acids (those that the body cannot synthesise and are available mainly in animal sources) and vitamin B_{12}. Consuming combinations such as corn and beans or rice and beans can provide all the essential amino acids required. Supplements may also be recommended in some instances.

13.2 Functions and classes of food

1 To supply energy for mechanical work of muscles, skeleton and heart, for protein synthesis, and to maintain body temperature (birds and mammals).
2 To provide for growth (increase in cell numbers) and repair of damaged tissue. The synthesis of DNA requires energy.
3 To maintain health and provide protection against disease.
4 To synthesise essential substances such as hormones and enzymes.

To perform the functions above, the body requires the following classes of food:

1 carbohydrates and fats for energy;
2 minerals and vitamins to maintain good health, assist or promote efficient metabolic activity and prevent deficiency diseases;
3 water (which makes up 65%–70% of body mass) to act as a solvent for biochemical reactions;
4 dietary fibre or roughage consisting of cellulose to maintain optimal muscular activity of the gut, reduce the risk of bowel cancer, and reduce blood cholesterol, thereby promoting cardiovascular health.

Maintaining a healthy diet is important in the prevention and treatment of physiological diseases such as hypertension and diabetes.

13.3 A balanced diet

A balanced diet should consist of foods from the following groups:

Table 13.1 *Food groups in a balanced diet*

Food group	Supplies	Examples
Staples	Carbohydrate, minerals, vitamins, dietary fibre	Rice, bread, yam, potato, cornmeal
Legumes	Carbohydrate, protein, dietary fibre	Gungo/pigeon peas, soya beans, peanuts, red/kidney beans, chick peas/channa
Dark green leafy and yellow vegetables	Vitamins, minerals, dietary fibre, water	Callaloo, bhagi, pakchoy, carrot, pumpkin
Animal products	Protein, fat	Meat, chicken, fish, eggs, cheese, milk
Fruits	Carbohydrate, vitamins, minerals, dietary fibre, water	Oranges, ripe bananas, mango, guava
Fats and fat substitutes	Fat, (vitamin A in enriched margarines)	Margarine, butter, oil, peanut butter, ackees

13.4 The energy value of food

We require energy for:

1 the **complete functioning** of the body (i.e. breathing, heart beat, blood circulation, maintenance of body temperature, excretion) which is called the basal metabolism;
2 our **work activities** (e.g. digging in the fields, writing at a desk, cleaning houses, working in a factory);
3 the **daily activities** that we perform apart from work (e.g. getting up, standing, washing, eating).

Energy requirements vary depending on age, sex and level of physical activity. Sedentary workers (teachers, clerks, tellers and cashiers) require less energy than labourers. Individuals who exercise regularly also require more energy. See Table 13.3 over the page.

Table 13.2 *Vitamins*

Vitamins	Source in food	Deficiency symptoms
A (retinol)	Eggs, milk, fish, liver, palm oil, green and yellow vegetables	Night blindness – poor night vision, flaky skin
B (thiamine, riboflavin)	Groundnuts, liver, palm oil, brown rice, tomatoes, milk and fish	Beriberi (disease of the nervous system), muscles weak and painful, weak heart
C (ascorbic acid)	Oranges, limes, cabbage, tomatoes, raw vegetables	Scurvy – bleeding from gums, breakdown of skin and blood vessels, wounds fail to heal
D (calciferol)	Fish oils, liver, eggs (also formed in human skin by action of sunlight and essential for calcium uptake)	Rickets (weak bones), poor teeth, osteomalacia in adults
E (tocopherol)	Green vegetables, liver, plant oils, margarine	Protects fatty acids and cell membranes from oxidation

Table 13.3 *Mineral elements*

Element	Source in food	Importance to body
Nitrogen	Meat, eggs, fish, milk	Synthesis of protein
Phosphorus	Meat, eggs, fish, milk	Synthesis of protein DNA and ATP, formation of teeth and bones
Iron	Liver, eggs, kidney, green vegetables	Formation of haemoglobin; absence causes iron deficiency anaemia
Calcium	Meat, milk, cheese, green vegetables	Formation of teeth and bones, blood clotting, absence causes rickets
Iodine	Sea fish and other sea foods, iodised table salt	Formation of thyroxine in thyroid gland, absence causes goitre (swelling of neck)
Sodium	Green vegetables, table salt	Maintenance of blood and tissue fluid, maintains water balance of cells, transmission of nerve impulses

Table 13.4 *Energy requirements*

	Calories per day
Normal, healthy male up to age 59:	2700–3000
Normal, healthy female up to age 59:	2200
Pregnant and nursing female:	2200 + (300–500)
Normal, healthy male adolescent:	2700–3000
Normal, healthy female adolescent:	2200

Carbohydrate, fat and protein all supply energy. Unused energy or that which is in excess of the body's requirement is stored as fat and so can lead to obesity. Obese individuals are at risk of developing hypertension (high blood pressure), heart disease and diabetes mellitus or type 2 diabetes.

To make our diet healthy we should eat small meals regularly – three or more times per day. We should eat more fruits, vegetables, wholegrains, lean meat and fish, and less fatty food, sugar and salt. We should also drink a lot of water.

14 Respiration

Respiration is a biochemical process that takes place in the cells of organisms. Enzymes catalyse the process. Glucose primarily, and other organic molecules are oxidised, producing energy as ATP.

Respiration is a chemical process and is not to be confused with breathing, which is a physical process or gas exchange (getting O_2 from the environment and releasing CO_2 into the environment).

14.1 Aerobic respiration

The complete oxidation of organic molecules (carbohydrates and fats) to yield a considerable amount of energy together with waste products, water and carbon dioxide, in the living cell. It begins in the cytoplasm, is completed in the mitochondria and is enzyme catalysed. Energy is stored in a compound called adenosine triphosphate (ATP).

$$\text{glucose + oxygen} \xrightarrow{\text{enzymes}} \text{carbon dioxide + water + energy}$$

ATP is formed from adenosine diphosphate (ADP) and phosphate. Breakdown or hydrolysis of ATP to ADP and phosphate releases energy quickly. ATP is the energy carrier in all living cells and so is referred to as the 'universal energy currency'. The rate of ATP formation and hydrolysis can be varied based on the requirements of the cell. Energy not transferred to ATP is lost as heat.

$$\text{Energy + ADP + phosphate} \longrightarrow \text{ATP}$$

The ATP releases energy when required:

$$\text{ATP} \longrightarrow \text{ADP + phosphate + energy}$$

14.2 Anaerobic respiration

This involves the incomplete oxidation of an organic molecule to yield a small amount of energy, ethanol and carbon dioxide. It occurs in the absence of oxygen in bacteria and fungi (e.g. in yeast cells, where it is called **fermentation**) and in humans (muscle cells).

In yeast cells:

$$\text{glucose} \xrightarrow{\text{enzymes}} \text{ethanol + carbon dioxide + energy}$$

In muscle cells:

$$\text{glucose} \xrightarrow{\text{enzymes}} \text{lactic acid + energy}$$

Note that anaerobic respiration is less efficient in energy production than aerobic respiration. Much energy is still stored in the intermediate breakdown products (ethanol or lactic acid), although ethanol produced by yeast cells cannot be further metabolised by these cells.

Fermentation is used in the production of bread, beer, wine, yoghurt, cheese, butter, cocoa and coffee. Yeast can be used to produce alcohol for alcoholic drinks when a sugary compound is fermented (e.g. grape juice for wine, barley for whiskey and molasses for rum). Yeast is also used by bakers to produce carbon dioxide gas in dough so that the bread is 'light' (full of holes formed by the gas).

Anaerobic respiration in humans supplies energy rapidly and when necessary, e.g. when an athlete runs a 400 m race. Oxygen does not arrive quickly enough for aerobic respiration so that anaerobic respiration occurs. The rate of ATP production in this instance is 2.5 times faster than aerobic respiration. Lactic acid builds up in the muscles and oxygen debt occurs. Rising levels of lactic acid during strenuous exercise results in muscle fatigue. The lactic acid can be oxidised later to produce energy when oxygen becomes available to the cells due to an increase in the rate and depth of breathing.

15 Gas exchange mechanisms

[syllabus sections B3.6 to 3.8]

Respiration requires oxygen and produces carbon dioxide. **Photosynthesis** requires carbon dioxide and produces oxygen. Gas exchange allows for the supply and removal of these gases. **Diffusion** is the physical process that facilitates gas exchange.

Characteristics of gas exchange surfaces

1 They are permeable so that gases can pass through.
2 They are thin because diffusion is efficient over distances of less than 1 mm.
3 They have a large surface area, because the larger the surface area, the faster the rate of diffusion.
4 In animals the surface has a good blood supply to bring carbon dioxide to the surface and remove oxygen.
5 In animals an efficient ventilation mechanism removes air with a high carbon dioxide concentration and replaces it with air of a high oxygen concentration.

15.1 Gaseous exchange organs

Flowering plants

Flowering plants respire **at all times**. They photosynthesise during daylight only. The net gas exchange between these two processes is that due to **faster photosynthesis in daylight:**

CO$_2$ is taken up and O$_2$ is produced.

At **night** when there is **no photosynthesis:**

O$_2$ is taken up and CO$_2$ is produced.

Gases are exchanged by diffusion through stomata in the leaves and green stems. In woody stems gas exchange takes place through cracks in the bark or slits called lenticels.

Root hairs are numerous, long and narrow, with thin permeable walls. Oxygen dissolved in soil water and in the air spaces between soil particles diffuses into the cytoplasm of the root hair, carbon dioxide moves in the opposite direction; both move along their respective concentration gradients.

Leaves are thin, have a large surface area relative to volume and are the main sites of gas exchange. Inside the leaves there are large air spaces between spongy mesophyll cells.

During the night, or when the plant is not photosynthesising, air containing a high concentration of oxygen diffuses through the sub-stomatal spaces and dissolves in the moisture on the walls of mesophyll cells and across the cell membrane. Carbon dioxide leaves by the same pathway, in the reverse order. During the day, when the plant is photosynthesising the opposite applies.

Fish

Gills form the gas exchange surface of the fish. Each gill consists of two rows of gill filaments. The **lamellae** (plates) of the gill filaments are very thin, have a large surface area and contain tiny blood vessels. They have a rich blood supply and diffusion is rapid from the water into the blood.

With **gill covers** closed, water passes through the mouth and into the buccal cavity and then enters the pharynx. When the mouth then closes, the gill covers open and the water passes out over the **gill arches** and

Fig. 15.1 *(a) Gaseous exchange through a single gill of a fish (b) Gaseous exchange in the human alveolus*

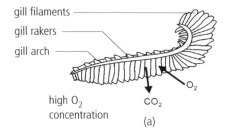

gill filaments
gill rakers
gill arch

high O$_2$ concentration

O$_2$

CO$_2$

(a)

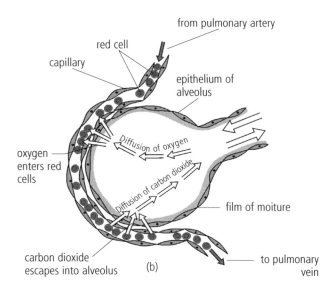

from pulmonary artery

red cell

capillary

epithelium of alveolus

Diffusion of oxygen

oxygen enters red cells

Diffusion of carbon dioxide

film of moisture

carbon dioxide escapes into alveolus

(b)

to pulmonary vein

Table 15.1 *Bones and muscles used to breathe*

	Inhalation (active process)	Exhalation (passive process)
External intercostal muscles	Contract	Relax
Internal intercostal muscles	Relax	Contract
Diaphragm	Contracts (flattens)	Relaxes (arches)
Rib cage	Moves up and out	Moves down and in
Pressure and volume changes	Volume increases, thus pressure decreases and air flows in	Volume decreases, thus pressure increases and air flows out
Alveoli	Inflated	Reduced volume

through the **gill slits**. Oxygen dissolved in the water diffuses into the blood capillaries and is taken up by the haemoglobin of the red blood cells.

Mammal

The gas exchange surface consists of air sacs or alveoli in the **lungs**. The two lungs are enclosed in an airtight **thoracic cavity**. The lungs are lined on the outside with a membrane that is continuous with the lining of the chest cavity – pleural membranes. Pleural fluid separates these two membranes. Air enters the nose and mouth and passes through the **buccal cavity, pharynx, larynx** (voice box) and finally into the **trachea**. The opening of the trachea is the **glottis** protected by the **epiglottis** that prevents the entry of food. Rings of cartilage support the trachea.

The trachea branches into two **bronchi**, each of which divides into many **bronchioles**. Each bronchiole ends in tiny sacs called **alveoli**. The walls of the air sacs are extremely thin (< 1.0 mm). When the air sacs are filled with air they enlarge and are round in shape. When air leaves, the air sacs are less round but never collapse. Blood capillaries form a network on the outer surface of the alveoli. (see Fig. 15.1(b)).

Ribs and muscles surround the lungs. The muscular diaphragm (Fig. 15.2) separates the thoracic from the abdominal cavity.

15.2 Breathing mechanism

The movement of the intercostal muscles and diaphragm changes the volume of the thoracic cavity, facilitating the movement of air in and out of the lungs.

15.3 Effects of cigarette smoking

Tar, carbon monoxide and nicotine are the components of cigarette smoke that threaten human health.
Tar – destroys the alveoli, reducing the surface area for

Fig. 15.2 *The human respiratory system*

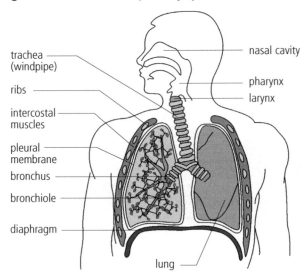

gas exchange, resulting in emphysema; contains carcinogens that induce uncontrolled cell division in the cells of the respiratory system causing cancer, which can spread from lungs to liver, adrenal glands and brain.
Carbon monoxide – binds irreversibly with haemoglobin (the oxygen transport pigment) so the blood carries less oxygen and so the cells receive less.
Nicotine – leads to physical and psychological dependence on cigarettes, stimulates the nervous system, increases the heart rate and blood pressure, and results in reduced blood supply to hands and feet.

Banning smoking in public places is widely advocated to reduce the negative effects of cigarette smoke on non-smokers (who are passive smokers).

Public education campaigns are also widely used to inform individuals of the negative effects of cigarette smoking. These involve the use of radio and television advertisements and billboards.

16 Transport

The smaller a living organism, the larger the surface area relative to the volume (surface area is greater than volume). As organisms increase in size the surface area relative to the volume is smaller (volume is greater than the surface area).

The increasing body size and complexity of plants and animals means that simple diffusion is not sufficient to provide materials or eliminate waste matter. Specialised transport systems are therefore required to move or circulate substances within living organisms.

16.1 Substances transported

Gases

Oxygen and carbon dioxide obtained from the atmosphere by land organisms, or in a dissolved state from water by aquatic organisms. Water vapour is liberated by land organisms.

Solutes

Useful and waste substances are transported. Organic molecules such as sucrose, urea, amino acids, proteins, hormones and inorganic molecules, mineral salts or ions such as chloride, potassium and sodium are transported in solution in plants and animals.

Water

The universal solvent in which the solutes listed above are transported. Plants take up soil water by osmosis.

16.2 Transport in vascular plants

The mass flow of substances within the conducting tissue (xylem and phloem) of vascular plants, water and ions through the xylem is called **translocation**. Ions and organic substances made in the leaves are carried by the phloem to growth regions (apices) of root and shoot and to storage organs.

16.3 Conducting tissue

See Figs. 16.1 and 16.2 showing the structure of xylem and phloem and the distribution of these tissues in the shoot and root of a dicotyledonous plant.

Root uptake

Root epidermis consists of specialised cells; root hairs that are elongated and so have a large surface area. Water passes through the freely permeable cell wall, crosses the cell membrane by osmosis and travels through the root cortex to the root xylem by osmosis. Mineral ions diffuse into root hairs and are also taken up by a process of active transport (movement of ions from a region of low to a region of high concentration through the cell membrane and requiring the use of energy as ATP).

Xylem

Xylem is the vascular tissue of plants consisting of vessels and tracheids. Both types of cell are dead and are

Fig. 16.1 *Vascular system of dicotyledonous plants*
(a) Phloem sieve tube element and companion cell (b) Xylem vessels

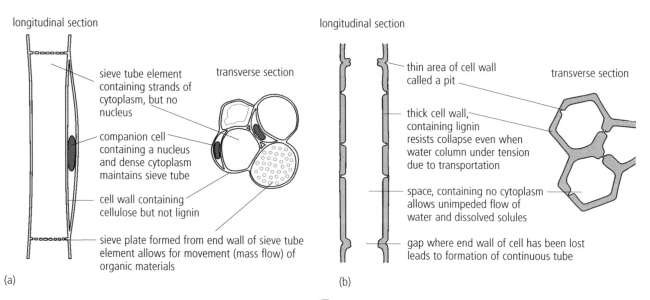

(a)

(b)

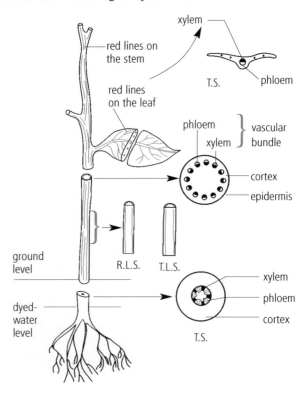

confined to vascular bundles. They conduct water and salts.

Xylem vessels form continuous, hollow tubes and are formed from cylindrical cells arranged end to end. During development the cells die; their walls become impregnated with lignin, a polymer. The end walls break down, forming hollow tubes with narrow lumens. Lignified walls contribute to significant tensile strength of these vessels so that they do not collapse. Mass flow of water for long distances is possible.

Phloem

Phloem is the vascular tissue of plants consisting of sieve tubes and companion cells. Sieve tubes are thin-walled, long cells connected at their end walls by sieve plates (pores in end walls). They have cytoplasm on the periphery but no nucleus. Sieve tubes translocate synthesised organic molecules (sugars and amino acids).

Companion cells are living cells with cytoplasm and nuclei. Numerous pores connect them to adjoining sieve tube elements. They carry out the metabolic activity necessary to maintain sieve tube elements.

16.4 Transpiration

Transpiration is the loss of water vapour from the surface of land plants, mainly through stomata but a small amount through the cuticle.

It occurs mostly during the day (when stomata are open for photosynthesis). The process of transpiration draws water and salts (as ions) up from the roots through the xylem (the transpiration stream). Water passes from the xylem in the leaves into the mesophyll cells. Water evaporates from the walls of mesophyll cells in leaves and diffuses as water vapour through air spaces via stomata to the exterior.

Excess water loss is harmful since it results in wilting (collapse of the plant) due to cell plasmolysis.

This movement up the xylem occurs by:

1   **Transpiration** – water lost from the leaves by transpiration pulls continuous, unbroken columns of water up the xylem; the columns of water are also under tension (transpiration pulling upards, gravity pulling downwards – the cohesion-tension theory). Water molecules also adhere to the internal walls of xylem – this too assists the upward movement of water.

2   **Root pressure** – due to entry of large amounts of water from soil into root hairs.

Rate of transpiration

Table 16.1 *The effect of external conditions and leaf structure on transpiration rate*

High rate	Low rate
High temperatures	Low temperatures
Low humidity of air	High humidity of air
Windy conditions	Little air movement
High light intensity – increases rate of photosynthesis and so water uptake	Low light intensity – decreases rate of photosynthesis and so water uptake
Ample soil water	Little soil water
Large number of stomata per unit area	Fewer stomata per unit area
Thin cuticle	Thick cuticle

16.5 Circulatory system in animals

The blood vascular system of vertebrates is described as a closed system and is made up of **vessels** (arteries, veins and capillaries, a **pump** (heart) and a **circulating fluid** (blood).

Table 16.2 Comparing arteries and veins

Arteries	Veins
Carry blood away from heart	Carry blood towards heart
Walls thick, elastic and muscular	Walls thinner, slightly muscular
Small internal diameter	Large internal diameter
Valves absent	Semilunar valves along length
Blood flow rapid	Blood flow slow
High blood pressure	Low blood pressure
Blood flow in pulses	Blood flow slow and steady
Lie deep in body (except radial artery in wrist and the carotid artery in the neck)	Lie near body surface
Blood oxygenated (except pulmonary artery)	Blood deoxygenated (except pulmonary vein)
Low volume of blood	Higher volume of blood

Some terms

Capillaries – very small blood vessels receiving blood from **arterioles** and passing it on to **venules**. Capillaries form a network in almost all vertebrate tissues. The walls are a single layer of flattened cells only. Water and dissolved substances from blood pass through capillary walls to become **tissue fluid**. Red blood cells and plasma proteins are retained in capillaries. Exchange of useful and waste materials takes place between the tissue fluid and cells. Leucocytes pass through capillary walls where they are required for action against bacteria. Tissue fluid, which now contains waste materials, passes into the **lymphatic**

Fig. 16.3 *(a) Cross-section of an artery (b) Cross-section of a vein (c) Cross-section of a capillary (d and e) Longitudinal section through a vein showing open and closed semilunar values*

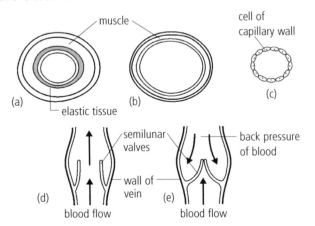

capillary, where it is called **lymph**. Lymphatic vessels return the lymph to the blood system by way of the subclavian veins near the heart.

Heart – a muscular pump; see Fig. 16.4 for structure.

Fig. 16.4 *Longitudinal section of a human heart, showing a passage of blood through the right and left sides of the heart*

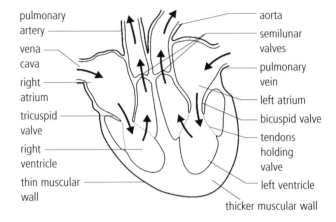

Action of heart – deoxygenated blood enters the **right atrium** via the anterior and posterior vena cava. Oxygenated blood enters the **left atrium** from the pulmonary vein. On contraction of the atria the blood is forced into the **right ventricle** through the tricuspid valve and into the **left ventricle** through the bicuspid value.

Systole – atria and ventricles contract. Blood is forced from atria into ventricles and from ventricles into the pulmonary artery and aorta. The return of blood to the atria on ventricular contraction is prevented by the closure of the tricuspid and bicuspid valves.

Diastole – when the heart muscles relax the cycle recommences.

Blood

Blood is composed of fluid (55%) and cells (45%).

Fluid

Plasma consists of approximately 95% water containing dissolved substances such as:

1. nutrients, e.g. glucose, amino acids, vitamins, fatty acids and glycerol;
2. ions, e.g. hydrogencarbonate, chloride, sodium, calcium and potassium;
3. hormones, e.g. insulin and thyroxine;
4. blood proteins, e.g. fibrinogen and prothrombin for blood clotting and enzymes;
5. excretory products, e.g. urea.

Fig. 16.5 *Diagram of the circulation of blood in humans*

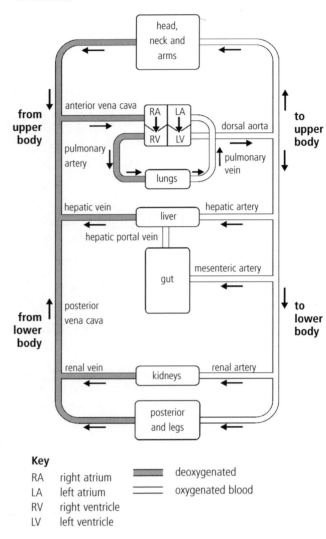

Key

RA	right atrium	▬▬	deoxygenated
LA	left atrium	══	oxygenated blood
RV	right ventricle		
LV	left ventricle		

Cells

Red blood cells (erythrocytes) constitute 45% of blood.

1 They have no nucleus and so can accommodate more haemoglobin.
2 Their biconcave disc shape exposes a large surface area for exchange of oxygen and is flexible enough to squeeze through narrow capillaries.
3 There are five million red blood cells per mm³ of blood.
4 They contain haemoglobin (an iron-containing protein), which reacts with oxygen to form oxyhaemoglobin.

5 They develop from cells in the bone marrow.
6 They have shorter lives (three months) because the nucleus is absent.
7 They are destroyed in the liver or spleen when no longer functional.

Fig. 16.6 *Red blood cells (erythrocytes) and white blood cells (leucocytes)*

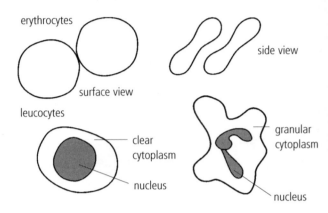

White blood cells (leucocytes) constitute less than 1% of blood. White blood cells have nuclei, a crawling motion (amoeboid) and occur at 10 000 per mm³ blood.

Platelets are membrane-bound cell fragments released from cells in the bone marrow. They have no nucleus and are essential for blood clotting.

Transport functions of blood

1 Red blood cells carry oxygen as oxyhaemoglobin from lungs to tissues where needed (respiring tissue).
2 Blood carries carbon dioxide from the tissues where it is produced (respiring tissue) in the form of hydrogencarbonate in plasma.
3 It carries digested food (glucose, amino acids), mineral salts (sodium, potassium) and vitamins (vitamin C) from the small intestine and liver to organs where these products are used or stored.
4 It carries hormones from the glands where it is transported to target cells, tissues or organs.
5 It carries blood proteins (fibrinogen, prothrombin, antibodies) to damaged tissue or sites of infection.
6 It carries excretory material (urea) in plasma from the liver to the kidneys.
7 Blood distributes heat from the liver and muscles.

16.6 Storage in living organisms

Stored food serves primarily as a reservoir of energy for future needs. It is used for metabolic activity associated with maintenance, growth and reproduction.

Autotrophs have no need to photosynthesise continuously because environmental conditions may not permit this, e.g. winter in temperate countries or drought in tropical countries.

Heterotrophs have no need to feed continuously because food may be scarce.

Sites and substances stored in plants

Seeds store minerals, e.g. phosphorus and vitamins. Fruits store starch, which is converted to sugars as fruit ripen; ripe fruits are eaten by animals and so the seeds are dispersed.

Starch and sugar reserves in storage organs are important for vegetative (asexual) reproduction.

Starch, proteins and oils stored in seeds are a reserve for the embryo. These are metabolised when the embryo begins to grow.

Sites of storage and substances stored in animals

Fats are stored:
1 around the intestines in mammals where they serve as an energy reserve;
2 in the skin (dermis) of mammals, providing insulation;
3 in the fat of hibernating animals as an energy reserve;
4 in the fat of blubber in whales and sea cows to provide buoyancy.

Glycogen is stored in the liver and muscles as an energy reserve, which is easily hydrolysed to glucose. Vitamins A, D, E and K, minerals, iron and potassium are also stored in the liver.

Table 16.3 *Types of white blood cell*

Cell	Nucleus	Cytoplasm	Function
Neutrophils 72%	Lobed	Granular	Engulf bacteria
Lymphocyte 24%	Round	Non–granular	Produce and release antibodies

Table 16.4 *Storage sites and substances stored in plants*

Storage structures and organs	Examples	Major substances stored
Stem tuber	Irish potato	Starch
Corm – underground stem tuber	Dasheen	Starch
Root tuber	Yam, sweet potato	Starch
Swollen tap root	Carrot	Sucrose
Bulb – fleshy leaves	Onion	Glucose
Stem	Sugar cane	Sucrose
Seed – cotyledons and endosperm	Kidney beans, Gungo/Pigeon peas	Starch
Seed – cotyledons	Soya bean and other legumes	Protein
Seed – kernel or endosperm	Coconut	Oil

17 Excretion

Excretion – this is the removal of waste products of metabolism from living organisms. If allowed to accumulate, the metabolic activity of living organisms is adversely affected.

17.1 Excretory products of plants

These are few because plants make only what they need.

1 **Carbon dioxide** produced during respiration. In light this gas is used in photosynthesis and in darkness it diffuses out of the leaf (see Respiration on p. 37).
2 **Oxygen** produced during photosynthesis diffuses out of the stomata during periods of light. Respiring plant parts utilise some oxygen.
3 Some waste material (e.g. **calcium oxalate**) is deposited in the cells while some, e.g. **tannins**, are deposited in bark, heartwood or leaves. When leaves fall the waste materials are removed. Wastes stored in bark and heartwood will not affect metabolic activity.

Water conservation in plants

Plants, like animals, must conserve water to survive in environments where water may be scarce and to avoid wilting. These adaptations may be structural or physiological and may include:

1 water storage roots – members of the pumpkin family (*Cucurbitaceae*) especially those growing in arid regions have water storage roots, some of which may weigh in excess of 25 kg;
2 deep root systems – e.g. Oleander and Acacia;
3 waxy cuticles and few stomata – e.g. prickly pear (*Opuntia*);
4 CAM photosynthesis – cacti and other succulents growing in warm, arid regions open their stomata only at night, taking in carbon dioxide during this period. During the day the stomata are closed and the carbon dioxide taken in at night is used to make organic molecules. Closure of the stomata during the day conserves water that would be lost because of transpiration.

17.2 Excretory products of animals

There are three main excretory products: carbon dioxide, water and nitrogenous compounds (mainly urea).

Excretion in mammals

Lungs – carbon dioxide and water are excreted by the lungs, diffused into the alveolar spaces and removed during exhalation. The carbon dioxide is produced by cellular respiration and travels in blood as hydrogen carbonate diffusing from capillaries surrounding alveoli, into alveolar space.

Skin – sweat secreted onto the skin evaporates from the surface of the skin. It consists of water, salts and a small quantity of urea.

Liver

1 Deamination of excess amino acids forms urea and some carbohydrates.
2 Breakdown of old red blood cells: haemoglobin from these cells is broken down to form the bile pigments, bilirubin and biliverdin.
3 Detoxification of poisons such as drugs, alcohol and nicotine.

Kidneys – excrete nitrogenous waste (urea mainly, uric acid, creatinine) and are responsible for regulating the concentration of body fluids, i.e. osmoregulation.

Kidneys: form and function

The **kidneys** are two bean-shaped, dark red organs lying in the dorsal side of the abdominal cavity. A fibrous capsule of connective tissue covers each kidney. Internally, each kidney has an outer cortex and an inner medulla. The kidney is composed of a mass of minute tubules called nephrons (kidney tubules) and numerous blood vessels (see Fig.17.1).

Fig. 17.1 *The human excretory system*

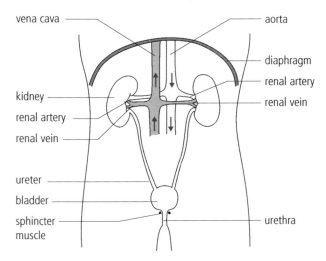

Tubes attached to each kidney

Renal artery – delivers blood to kidney.
Renal vein – takes blood away from the kidney.
Ureter – delivers urine from kidney to bladder.
Urethra – takes urine away from the bladder.

Each **nephron** begins at a **renal capsule** (cup-shaped and hollow) and from this leads to a long tubule ending at the collecting duct. The tubule is divided into three distinct regions:

1 the first convoluted tubule;
2 the loop of Henlé;
3 the second convoluted tubule.

Each part of the nephron is supplied with blood by means of capillaries (see Fig. 17.2).

Fig. 17.2 *Kidney tubule (nephron)*

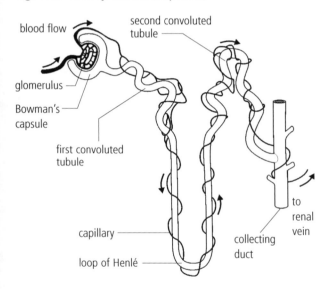

Function of the kidneys

Ultrafiltration. A knot of capillaries in the renal capsule, called the **glomerulus**, has an arteriole that brings blood from the renal artery. This is wider than the arteriole that leaves the renal capsule. This produces a pressure greater than normal blood pressure and forces some of the plasma (together with dissolved substances) through the capillary walls and into the renal capsule. Large blood protein molecules and red blood cells do not normally pass into the capsule. The fluid present in the renal capsule is called the **glomerular filtrate**.
Selective reabsorption takes place in the first convoluted tubule where all of the glucose and amino acids, most of the water, sodium, chloride, potassium,

and 40%–50% of the urea are absorbed from the filtrate.

In the loop of Henlé salts are secreted from the tubule into the surrounding tissue. Water consequently leaves by osmosis. In mammals the reabsorption of water takes place in the second convoluted tubule and collecting duct; this is an osmoregulatory process.

Reabsorption of water from the glomerular filtrate produces urine that consists of 95% water, 2.0% urea, 0.35% sodium, 0.6% chloride, 0.05% uric acid, and 0.075% creatinine. Any glucose appearing in the urine is a symptom of the disease called **diabetes mellitus** (sugar diabetes). Diabetes may be of two types:

1 Type 1 diabetes (insulin dependent diabetes) – the islets of Langerhans in the pancreas do not produce enough insulin to regulate the concentration of blood glucose, so any excess is secreted in the urine. Weight loss and dehydration result.
2 Type 2 diabetes (non-insulin dependent diabetes) – adequate insulin is produced but the cells fail to take up glucose in response to the hormone.

Osmoregulation and homeostasis in animals

Osmoregulation is the maintenance of correct levels of water and salts in animals so that the appropriate blood concentration can be controlled. This is an example of a homoeostatic process. **Homeostasis** is the ability of an organism to maintain a constant internal environment, i.e. in this context to keep the tissue fluids unchanged in terms of pH and temperature.

Homeostatic control methods are automatic and self-adjusting. They function like controls on machines, e.g. the thermostat on an electric oven. Change in the normal levels of a component of tissue fluid is detected by receptors of the nervous system and sent to control centres in the brain, which bring about corrective action. This results in an increase or decrease of the factor to bring it back to the norm (normal). This is called negative feedback (see Fig. 17.3). If there is a complete breakdown and the organism is unable to restore the situation then the change continues to increase or decrease. This is called positive feedback, and it often means that a bad situation is made worse. Fortunately this is rare in nature, but if it does proceed unchecked then it could result in death (see Fig. 20.3 on p. 55).

Fig. 17.3 *Homeostasis*

Water regulation in humans

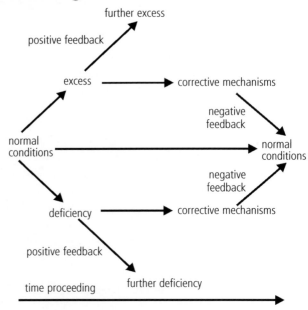

further excess

positive feedback

excess → corrective mechanisms

negative feedback

normal conditions → normal conditions

negative feedback

deficiency → corrective mechanisms

positive feedback

time proceeding   further deficiency

In humans, the body cannot afford to lose all of the water that passes into the nephrons, so 99% of it is reabsorbed. When the body is short of water, i.e. when the blood is concentrated, more water is reabsorbed and less released. When there is too much water, i.e. when the blood is dilute, less water is reabsorbed and more released. Thus a constant water balance is maintained in the body.

Antidiuretic hormone (ADH) controls this process and is secreted into the blood stream by the **pituitary gland**, found in the brain, when blood becomes more concentrated, e.g. due to excessive water loss because of sweating, diarrhoea and the intake of very salty foods. This is sensed by osmoreceptors in the hypothalamus so that ADH is secreted. ADH stimulates the second convoluted tubule and collecting duct to absorb more water from the filtrate, producing a small volume of concentrated urine.

If blood becomes less concentrated due to a large intake of water or reduced sweating, this is sensed by osmoreceptors in the hypothalamus so that less ADH is secreted. Less water will be reabsorbed from the filtrate, producing a large volume of dilute urine.

Diabetes insipidus is a condition in which insufficient ADH is secreted so that large quantities of dilute urine are produced.

High blood pressure (hypertension), atherosclerosis and diabetes often lead to chronic kidney failure, which gradually sets in over a number of years.

Treating kidney failure is expensive, involving dialysis or kidney transplant surgery. Preventing renal failure is therefore of major importance.

18 Skeleton and movement

[syllabus sections B6.1 to 6.6]

Plants and animals show **movement**, that is, the **change in position** of one structure relative to another (plants and fungi move only by growing).

Plant movements are induced by external stimuli and are called **tropic movements** or **tropisms**. Growth in the direction of a stimulus is described as being positive, and away as negative. Accordingly, shoots are positively phototropic growing towards light and negatively geotropic, growing away from the force of gravity. Roots are negatively phototropic but positively geotropic. Tropic responses in plants are controlled by auxins. Animals show **locomotion**, i.e. the **movement of the whole organism** from one place to another.

Animals move to find food and mates, to escape predators and to find favourable habitats.

Table 18.1 *Plant and animal movement*

Animals	Plants
Locomotion	No locomotion (except very simple unicellular plants)
(a) food-seeking (heterotrophs)	(a) produce their own food (autotrophs)
(b) mate-seeking (sexual reproduction)	(b) produce reproductive structures with dispersal of pollen and fruits by outside agencies

18.1 Types of locomotory mechanisms in animals

1 **Pseudopodia** or 'false feet' – *Amoeba*, a unicellular organism, moves by producing flowing projections of the cytoplasm that pull the organism forward in the direction of travel.
2 **Cilia or flagella** – hair-like projections on the surface of cells, which beat in a coordinated rhythm, propelling unicellular organisms forward. Cilia are short and found in organisms such as *Paramecium*. Flagella are longer and are found in sperm cells, some bacteria and *Euglena*.
3 **Skeleton and muscles**
   (a) **Exoskeleton** (e.g. insects, crabs and spiders) – hard outer covering called cuticle, which contains **chitin**. The skeleton is jointed with flexible membranes. Limbs are hollow and have a series of hinge joints with internal muscle attachment.
   (b) **Endoskeleton** (fish, amphibians, birds, reptiles and mammals) – composed of

cartilage and bone. The skeleton is jointed with bones and joints internal to the muscles.
   (c) **Hydrostatic skeleton** (earthworm) – consists of a fluid-filled body cavity enclosed by a muscular body wall. Pressure on the fluid is increased by contraction of circular muscles. Alteration between the contraction of circular and longitudinal muscles propels the worm along.

18.2 The human skeleton

Functions

1 **Support** – raises the body off the ground to allow movement; maintenance of shape; suspends the soft parts.
2 **Protection** – of internal organs (skull protects the brain, ribcage protects heart and lungs).
3 **Movement** – provides attachment for muscles; bones serve as levers on which muscles act for greater efficiency.
4 **Production of blood cells** in bone marrow.
5 **Provision of calcium and phosphorus reserves** in bone.

Main parts of the skeleton

Axial skeleton

(skull, vertebral column, ribs and sternum)
The skull consists of the **cranium** that protects the brain, two sockets for eyes, two ear capsules and the jaws. The lower jaw is moveable to allow the chewing of food and speech. The vertebral column has **vertebrae** for protecting the spinal cord, attachment of muscles and the maintenance of body position. Discs of cartilage separate these. Ribs are attached to the thoracic vertebrae, enabling the rib cage to move up and down during breathing movements.

Fig. 18.1 *Anterior view of a generalised vertebra*

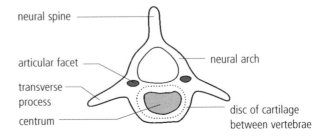

Table 18.2 *Human vertebrae*

Vertebrae (type and characteristic)	Number	Function
Cervical – small processes, head, vertebroarterial canal	7	1st atlas: nodding; 2nd axis: rotation; 3rd to 7th for twisting the neck
Thoracic – long neural spine, extra articulating facets for ribs	12	Jointed with ribs allowing breathing movements of thorax. Give some flexibility of body movement.
Lumbar – large transverse processes, large neural spine, extra projections for muscle attachment	5	Many muscles attached and they suffer considerable stress in locomotion and support. Allow backward bending of trunk, also sideways and twisting movements.
Sacral – fused vertebrae (to each other and to pelvic girdle)	5	Thrust of leg movements transmitted through pelvic girdle to vertebral column.
Caudal – (coccyx) no processes	5	No known function in humans

Appendicular skeleton (limbs and limb girdles)

Limb girdles

Pectoral girdle – not fused to vertebrae, attached only by tendons and muscles.

Pelvic girdle – fused to sacral vertebrae and thus transmits thrust of legs to vertebrae and body.

You must be able to draw, label and annotate simple diagrams of the long bones of a forelimb (the arm) or a hindlimb (the leg).

Limbs

Forelimbs (arms) and hindlimbs (legs) are based on the pentadactyl plan. Human limbs are unspecialised compared with those of the dog, whale, horse and cow and show the basic plan of limb structure.

Fig. 18.2 *Plan view of a generalised mammalian limb (the pentadactyl plan)*

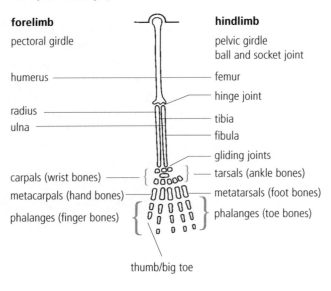

Fig. 18.3 *Bones of the forelimb (a) left humerus (anterior view) (b) left humerus (posterior view) (c) radius and ulna*

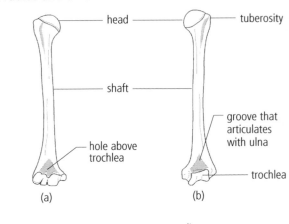

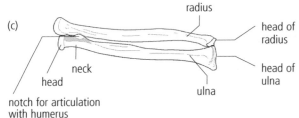

Fig. 18.4 *Bones of the hindlimb (a) left femur (anterior view) (b) left tibia and fibula*

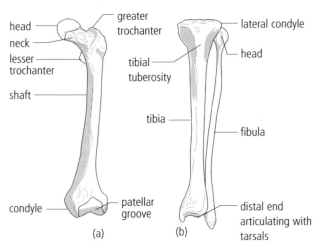

All vertebrae, long bones and girdles should be studied and drawn during practical work. You must also be able to distinguish between cervical, thoracic and lumbar vertebrae.

Joints

The skeleton is moved by muscular contraction on bones acting through joints. The types of joint are:

1 **immovable or suture joints** – the fixed joints (e.g. in the cranium or skull and pelvis);
2 **slightly movable bones** are bridged by cartilage (e.g. in the vertebral column), which provides flexibility, and by intervertebral discs;
3 **moveable joints**
   (a) **gliding joints** where two surfaces slide over each other (e.g. vertebrae, wrist, ankle);
   (b) **synovial joints** such as **ball and socket** joints that allow movement in all directions (e.g. shoulder and hip) and **hinge joints** that allow movement in one plane only (e.g. elbow and knee). The ends of the bones of these joints are capped with cartilage and are located within a synovial capsule filled with synovial fluid. The joints are strengthened by ligaments.

Fig. 18.5 *Section through: (a) a hinge joint and (b) a ball and socket joint*

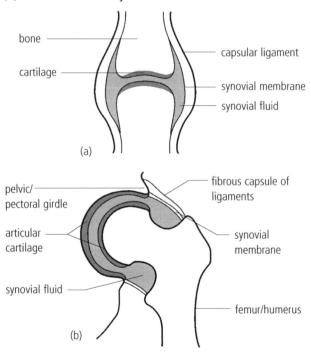

Muscles

Muscles are composed of fibres that contract and relax. They only act by 'pulling' and since they cannot 'push', they must work in pairs. While one muscle contracts the other relaxes; the action is reversed for movement in the opposite direction. The end of the muscle that remains relatively fixed is called the **origin**, the end that moves is called the **insertion**. For example, the origin of the biceps is on the shoulder and its insertion is on the radius. The contraction of the biceps moves the radius towards the shoulder.

The pairs of muscles are **antagonistic**. This means that one of the pair contracts and bends the limb (flexor muscle) while the other contracts and straightens the limb (extensor muscle).

Fig. 18.6 *The lever action of the human forelimb; (b) shows how the forearm is flexed when lifting a load.*

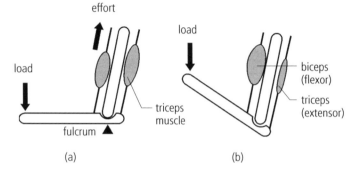

Types of muscles

1 **Skeletal, voluntary or striated muscle** is attached to bones by tendons and is under our voluntary control. Striated muscle consists of many cells called muscle fibres, which are cylindrical and long, each having a nucleus.
2 **Involuntary or unstriped muscle** is not under our voluntary control and is found in internal organs (e.g. iris of the eye, gut, bladder and blood vessels). These muscles also work in an antagonistic fashion (i.e. using circular and longitudinal muscles).
3 **Cardiac muscle** contracts continuously from before birth until death.

Tendons

Tendons are composed of inelastic fibrous tissue; they resist pulling strains. They attach muscle to bone and transmit the force of contraction of muscle to the bone. This permits a muscle to act at some distance from the bone that it moves (e.g. muscles on the forearm move the fingers because these muscles are attached by long tendons to the bones of the fingers).

Ligaments

These are tough but flexible and consist of inelastic white fibrous tissue. Ligaments join bones at joints and provide a capsule. This prevents dislocation at the joint and also confines movement to certain planes.

19 Response and coordination

19.1 Some terms

Stimulus – a change in the external or the internal environment of an organism, which brings about a response in that organism.

Response – a change in the activity of a part or the whole of the organism, which results from a stimulus.

19.2 Response in plants

Plants respond to stimuli (**light** and **gravity**) by the release of a chemical substance (**auxin**), which results in a growth response. This substance is produced at the apices (tips) of shoots and young leaves. It diffuses through the plant tissue and can be transported in the phloem. Its action is to stimulate growth by increasing the elongation of those cells that are found immediately behind the tip. In roots, the reverse action may occur (decreasing cell elongation).

These growth responses are called **tropisms** and their direction is determined by the direction of the stimulus.

> Growth towards the stimulus is positive.
> Growth away from the stimulus is negative.

The term 'tropism' is prefixed by the stimulus involved (e.g. light: **phototropism**; gravity: **geotropism**). Growth of a shoot towards light is called **positive phototropism**. Auxins in the shoot migrate away from light promoting elongation of cells on the non-illuminated side so that the stems grow in the direction of the light. Shoots are positively phototropic and negatively geotropic. Some roots are negatively phototropic; all are positively geotropic.

The phototropic response allows for greater exposure of shoots to available light for optimal photosynthetic activity. The geotropic response allows roots to grow down toward the ground or soil for anchorage, water and mineral elements.

19.3 Response in invertebrates

Plant response to stimuli also involves the growth response. Growth-regulating substances in the plant are called **auxins** and the most common of these is called **indoleacetic acid (IAA)**. Auxins are produced at root and shoot tips. When shoot tips are subjected to one-sided light the auxin accumulates on the dark side and increases cell division and elongation so that the shoot grows towards the light. In roots that are placed horizontally, the auxin accumulates on the underside of the root, inhibiting division and elongation so that the root grows downwards.

The same auxin increases growth in the shoot and inhibits growth in the root (see Fig. 19.1).

Organisms such as the earthworm, millipede and woodlouse show behaviour associated with the movement of the whole organism in relation to stimuli such as light, temperature and moisture. The central nervous system controls the reception of stimuli, transmission of nervous impulses and the action (response). The movement of the organism is called a **taxis** and it is a response to a directional stimulus. As with tropisms, these can be positive (towards) or negative (away from) and the stimuli can be light, chemicals or water. Thus woodlice move away from light, as do earthworms, millipedes and cockroaches. These organisms exhibit **negative phototaxis**. Some flying insects fly towards lights, exhibiting **positive phototaxis.** Mosquito repellents are effective because the response of the mosquitoes to the chemical is an example of negative chemotaxis.

Earthworms avoid desiccation by burrowing into moist soil and away from bright light, as do millipedes and woodlice. This response also allows these organisms to avoid predators.

Table 19.1 *Differences between plant and animal responses*

Plant	Animal
Receptors (root and shoot tips)	Receptors (eyes, antennae, ears, nose, skin)
No nervous system	Nervous system
Slow response	Fast response
Response by growth	Response by effectors giving movement or glandular secretion
Result is permanent change	Result is temporary change
Coordination by growth regulators	Coordination by nerves and hormones

The nervous and endocrine systems coordinate and control all the activities taking place within the animal body. These activities are responses to stimuli received from internal and external environments. These two systems are the link between stimulus and response and contribute to the survival and the maintenance of homeostasis of the organism.

Control by the nervous system involves the transmission of electrochemical impulses along nerves, which we examine later. Control by the endocrine system is exercised by chemicals (hormones), released

Fig. 19.1 *(a) Phototropism – action of auxin on a coleoptile and geotropism – action of auxin on (b) shoot and (c) root*

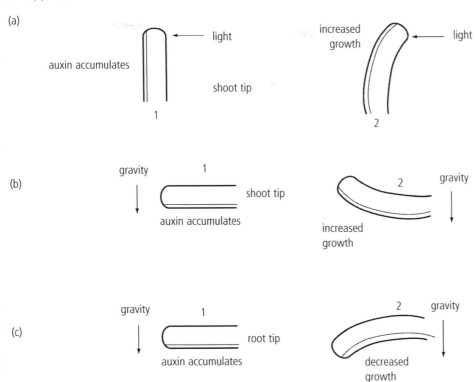

into the blood stream, which we examine in Chapter 21.

19.4 Nervous system

This is a network of cells enabling rapid response to changes in the environment. The following are essential.

Receptor – the organ or cell of an animal that detects a stimulus and initiates a nerve impulse.

Conductor – specialised conductor cells (neurones) transmit nerve impulses by electrochemical methods. There are three types of neurone: sensory, effector and connector.

Effector – the organ or cell (muscle or gland) of an animal that responds to a stimulus or the arrival of a nerve impulse.

The relationship between receptor and effector is as follows:

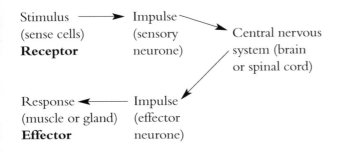

The nervous system is arranged in the following manner:

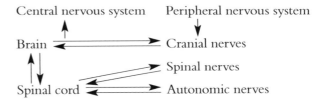

The central nervous system consists of the brain and spinal cord. Three protective membrane layers, called **meninges**, surround the brain. These meninges lie inside the bony cranium.

The brain

The brain consists of the major regions described below.

Cerebrum

The cerebrum contains the outer cortex (grey matter) that consists of cell bodies of neurones and is folded on its surface. The inner part (white matter) is formed from axons or neurones. Sensory areas of the cerebrum control smell, sight, hearing and skin sensations. Motor areas control muscles of the arms, legs, eyes and hands. The cerebrum is also concerned with voluntary behaviour, learning and memory.

Fig. 19.2 *(a) Effector neurone (b) Connector neurone (c) Sensory neurone*

Fig. 19.3 *(a) Longitudinal section of the human brain (b) Motor and sensory area of the cerebrum*

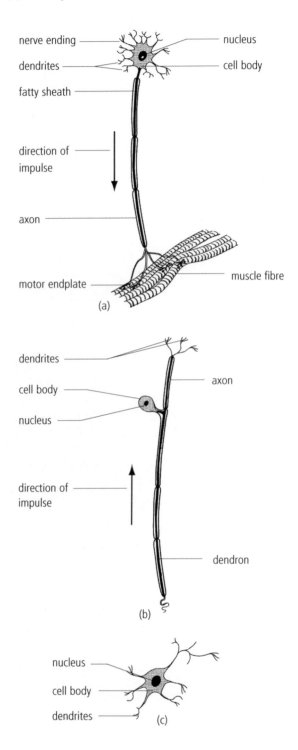

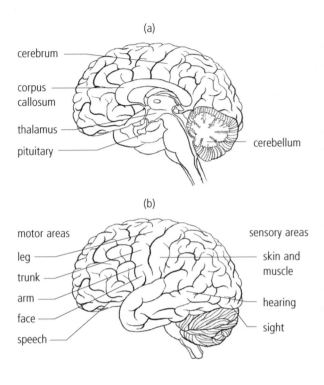

Cerebellum

Is concerned with the muscular coordination of the body including balance, posture and locomotion. Receives sensory impulses from muscles and eyes and sends motor impulses to skeletal muscles.

Medulla oblongata

Blood pressure, coughing, swallowing, yawning and sneezing are controlled from the medulla oblongata, a reflex centre. It coordinates breathing and the heart rate.

The spinal cord

The spinal cord is protected by the meninges and vertebrae. It serves to connect the brain with the peripheral nerves. For the structure of the spinal cord see Fig. 19.4 on p. 53.

Peripheral nervous system

The peripheral nervous system includes the cranial nerves, spinal nerves and autonomic nerves. Each of these three is composed of neurones (see Fig. 19.2 for neurone structure).

Cranial nerves

Twelve pairs of cranial nerves are attached to the brain. Some are sensory (impulses from eyes, ears and nose),

Hypothalamus

Regulates some aspects of homeostasis, coordinates the autonomic nervous system; regulates hunger, sleep, thirst, body temperature, water balance, blood pressure and controls the pituitary gland.

Temperature control and carbon dioxide levels in the blood are among the homeostatic mechanisms controlled from the hypothalamus (a reflex centre).

Fig. 19.4 *A spinal reflex arc*

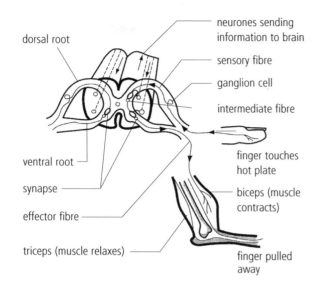

- dorsal root
- neurones sending information to brain
- sensory fibre
- ganglion cell
- intermediate fibre
- ventral root
- finger touches hot plate
- synapse
- biceps (muscle contracts)
- effector fibre
- triceps (muscle relaxes)
- finger pulled away

Fig. 19.5 *A cranial reflex arc*

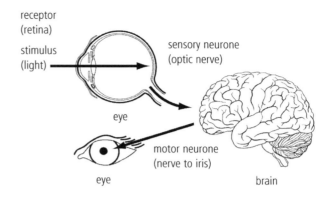

- receptor (retina)
- stimulus (light)
- sensory neurone (optic nerve)
- eye
- motor neurone (nerve to iris)
- eye
- brain

High light intensity: circular muscles contract
Low light intensity: radial muscles contract

some are effector (impulses to eye and tongue muscles), and some are mixed (impulses to and from the face).

Spinal nerves

Spinal nerves occur at regular intervals along the spinal cord. These are mixed (sensory and effector) receiving sensory impulses from the body and sending out impulses to muscles and glands. They are connected in the spinal cord by connector neurones and secondary neurones passing up and down the cord.

Autonomic nerves

Autonomic nerves are connected to each spinal nerve and control the internal (involuntary) activities of the gut and glands. This system of nerves is composed of the sympathetic and parasympathetic systems. These two systems tend to have opposing functions, but both are concerned with the workings of internal organs of the body (e.g. heart, lungs, gut, kidney, bladder etc.). The effectors are mostly involuntary muscle. For example, in the gut the sympathetic system inhibits peristalsis and the secretion of gut juices, whereas the parasympathetic stimulates peristalsis and secretion of gut juices.

Reflex action

A reflex action is a simple form of behaviour in an animal in which a stimulus causes a specific, simple response (e.g. a finger touching a hot plate is immediately withdrawn by contraction of the arm muscle; see Fig. 19.4) The constancy of the response depends upon a nervous pathway, called the **reflex arc**, along which the impulses travel.

Spinal reflex action

The simplest spinal reflex arc involves three neurones (sensory, intermediate, motor, see Fig. 19.4). Another example is the knee jerk reflex, i.e. if one knee is crossed over the other and the top knee is tapped just below the patella, the upper leg extends (straightens). Spinal reflex actions involve transmission of impulses along spinal nerves.

Cranial reflex action

A simple reflex involving the brain rather than the spinal cord. Examples are the blinking action of the eye when an object approaches, or the adjustment of the iris to light intensity. In both examples, the receptor is the retina and the effector is the muscle action of muscles of the eyelid or the muscles of the iris. Cranial reflex actions involve transmission of impulses along cranial nerves.

All simple reflex arcs allow the body of the animal to make automatic adjustments to change in the environment (stimuli). These may be
(a) internal, when the autonomic nerves are largely involved (e.g. blood pressure, breathing rate);
(b) external, when the spinal or cranial nerves may be involved (e.g. balance, blinking, iris, salivation).

20 Sense organs

Sense organs transfer the energy of a stimulus to the energy of nerve impulses that the brain interprets.

Major sense organs and the stimuli to which they respond are:
- the eye (sight organ) – light stimuli;
- the skin – mechanical and thermal stimuli of touch, heat, cold, pressure;
- the ear (sound and balance organ) – stimuli of sound, gravity;
- the tongue (taste organ) – chemical stimuli;
- the nose (olfactory organ) – chemical stimuli.

In this chapter we look at the eye and the skin.

20.1 Eye

For the structure of the eye see Fig. 20.1.

Functioning of the eye

Light enters through the transparent **conjunctiva** and **cornea**. Major focusing of the image occurs through the curved cornea. Light passes through the jelly–like **aqueous humour** of the front chamber of the eye to the pupil. The pupil size adjusts the amount of light entering the eye (see Fig. 19.5). Light now reaches the **lens**, which, at rest, is focused on distant objects. As light rays approach the eye, the lens becomes rounded or thick to ensure precise focusing of the image on the retina by contraction of the **ciliary muscles**. Light passes on through to the posterior chamber of the eye, filled with vitreous humour, and is finally focused on the light-sensitive retina. The fovea is an area of acute

or sharp vision in the centre of the retina. The retina has two types of cells:
1. cones to detect colour in bright light; and
2. rods to detect light strength (or black and white vision) in dim light.

The blind spot has no rods or cones since it is the point at which nerve fibres pass through the retina. The activity of the eye involves:
1. the alteration in pupil size to adjust light strength; and
2. the alteration in shape of the lens according to the distance of the object from the eye.

These two features together are called **accommodation** – the reflex adjustment to the shape of the lens allowing images of objects at various distances to be formed on the retina. As individuals age the lens loses its ability to become rounded and focus on near objects, so these persons will often require corrective lenses.

Humans have eyes on each side of the face. When both are trained on the same object, each eye sees the object from a slightly different angle, allowing us to perceive three-dimensional images and a sense of depth; this is binocular vision.

Sight defects

Persons who can see near objects but who do not see a size 20 letter 20 feet away easily are **short-sighted** or near-sighted. They have an elongated eyeball and need corrective lenses, which cause the light rays to bend

Fig. 20.1 *A diagram of a vertical section through the eyeball*

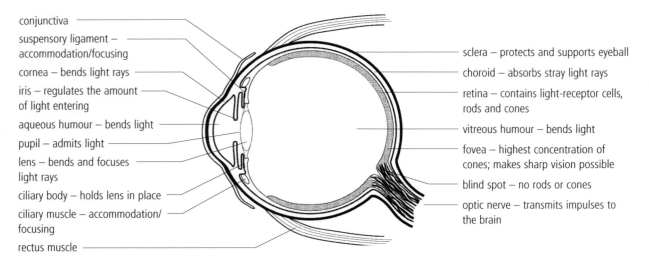

conjunctiva

suspensory ligament – accommodation/focusing

cornea – bends light rays

iris – regulates the amount of light entering

aqueous humour – bends light

pupil – admits light

lens – bends and focuses light rays

ciliary body – holds lens in place

ciliary muscle – accommodation/focusing

rectus muscle

sclera – protects and supports eyeball

choroid – absorbs stray light rays

retina – contains light-receptor cells, rods and cones

vitreous humour – bends light

fovea – highest concentration of cones; makes sharp vision possible

blind spot – no rods or cones

optic nerve – transmits impulses to the brain

slightly outwards (diverging lenses) before reaching the lens of the individual.

Persons who can see a size 20 letter 20 feet away but who cannot see near objects are described as being **long–sighted** or far–sighted. They may have a short eyeball and need corrective lenses that cause light rays to bend slightly inwards (converging lenses) before reaching the lens of the individual.

Fig. 20.2 *(a) Short-sightedness and its correction (b) Long-sightedness and its correction*

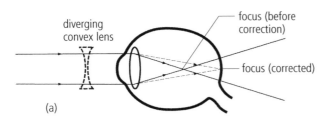

(a)

Cataract is caused by a clouding of the lens, which

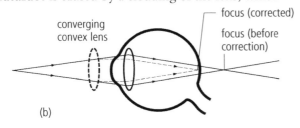

(b)

prevents light from passing through. Eventually the lens can be removed and correction applied by very strong lenses in front of the eye.

Glaucoma is a condition in which loss of vision occurs because of an abnormally high pressure in the eye. The aqueous humour produced by the ciliary body normally leaves the anterior cavity by tiny ducts. When these ducts are blocked, the aqueous humour builds up, pressure increases within the eyeball and compresses the arteries supplying the nerve fibre of the retina. This nerve fibre degenerates due to a lack of nutrients causing deterioration of sight (and blindness) over time. Surgery and special eye drops are necessary to treat the condition.

20.2 Skin and body temperature regulation in mammals

The skin is sensitive to touch, temperature and pressure, any of which can cause a pain sensation. The sense organs involved are sensory endings of nerves that are in the dermis, recognisable by their structure. Some have free nerve endings and are sensitive to the touch, pressure and pain, while others in a capsule (Pacinian corpuscle) are sensitive to touch and pressure.

Poikilothermic animals (fishes, amphibians,

reptiles) have body temperatures that vary with that of the environment. **Homoiothermic** mammals, including humans, maintain a constant body temperature and are fairly independent of enviromental temperature in accordance with the principle of homeostasis, which we introduced in an earlier chapter. We maintain a more or less constant body temperature by balancing heat production and heat loss, important aspects of which occur through the skin.

Heat production

Sources of heat in the body include:
- heat released in the tissues in oxidation processes;
- heat from the sun;
- heat from hot food and drink; and
- heat from hot baths.

Fig. 20.3 *Temperature ranges for body temperature in humans*

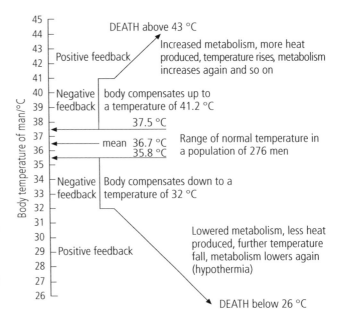

Heat loss

Heat is lost principally by:
- radiation from the body to cooler surroundings, which accounts for 55% of total heat loss;
- evaporation of water from the skin (sweat) and lungs (water vapour) when internal or external temperatures are high, which accounts for 27% of total heat loss (cats and dogs only have sweat glands in the skin of their paws only and so must breathe quickly to lose heat in water vapour leaving the lungs);
- convection, when warm air surrounding the skin moves away to be replaced by cooler molecules (15% of heat loss).

To a lesser extent we lose heat:
- via conduction because air doesn't conduct heat well;
- when we breathe colder air;
- when we excrete warm urine and faeces.

Sweat secretion is regulated by the **hypothalamus**, the temperature receptor and regulating centre in the brain, which aims to maintain a relatively constant optimum temperature of 37°C in humans. Blood temperature and impulses sent from hot and cold receptors in the skin stimulate the hypothalamus. Impulses are then conducted from the hypothalamus to the blood vessels and sweat glands in the skin. As blood vessels dilate and more blood flows through the skin, the temperature rises, permitting heat loss from the skin via radiation, and sweat secretion as a result of the larger supply of blood to the sweat glands. Sweat evaporation cools the body.

The role of hormones

Hormones produced by the thyroid gland and the adrenal medulla stimulate heat production. When it gets colder, more thyroxin and adrenal medulla hormones are secreted.

Table 20.1 *Physiological methods of controlling body temperature*

Methods of heat loss	Method of heat gain or retention
Increased sweating	Decreased sweating
Vasodilation or widening of blood vessels (more blood to the body surface, which releases heat and increases radiation and convection)	Vasoconstriction or constriction of blood vessels (less blood to body surface which decreases radiation and convection)
Hair lowered or flattened to decrease insulating air layer	Hair raised (traps more air for insulation but causes only 'goose flesh' in humans)
Decreased metabolism (less activity so less heat is produced)	Increased metabolism (more activity so more heat is produced)
Seasonal moult loses hair	Thicker coat of fur in winter or in cold climates

21 Endocrine glands and growth

[syllabus sections B7.12 to 7.13; B8.1 to 8.2]

The position of endocrine glands in humans is shown in Fig. 21.1 on p. 58.

Table 21.1 *Endocrine glands and their functions*

Gland	Position	Hormone secreted	Effect of hormone
Anterior pituitary	Base of brain	Thyroid stimulating hormone – TSH	Growth of thyroid gland
		Follicle stimulating hormone – FSH	Controls egg and sperm production
		Luteinising hormone – LH Ovulation in females; production of testosterone in males	
		Growth hormone	Growth, especially of limb bones; increased cell division and protein synthesis
Posterior pituitary	Base of brain	Anti-diuretic hormone – ADH	Removal of water from urine regulating concentration of blood
Thyroid	Neck	Thyroxine	Increases basal metabolic rate, heart rate and temperature regulation; growth and development
Islets of Langerhans	Pancreas	Insulin	Regulates blood glucose level by converting glucose to glycogen when blood glucose levels rise above normal
		Glucagon	Regulates blood glucose level by converting stored glycogen to glucose when levels of blood glucose fall below normal
Adrenals	Above kidneys	Adrenaline	Prepares body for action 'fight' or 'flight' by increasing heart rate and conversion of glycogen to glucose
Testes	Scrotum	Testosterone	Growth and development of male sex organs, muscle development, deepening of voice, hair in pubic region, on face, chest and in armpits, attraction to opposite sex
Ovary	Lower abdomen	Oestrogen	Regulates menstrual cycle, maintains pregnancy, develops breasts, hair in pubic region and armpits, widening of hips, attraction to opposite sex
		Progesterone	Regulates menstrual cycle, maintains pregnancy, develops breasts and pubic hair, works along with oestrogen to maintain oviducts, uterus and vagina

Fig. 21.1 *Position in the body of endocrine (ductless) glands*

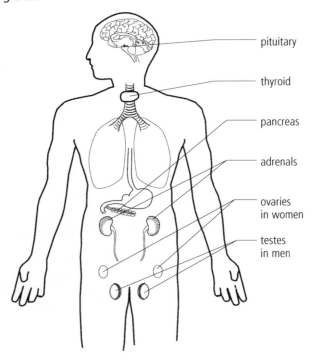

- pituitary
- thyroid
- pancreas
- adrenals
- ovaries in women
- testes in men

Fig. 21.2 *Growth curve of a population of animals such as a herd of deer*

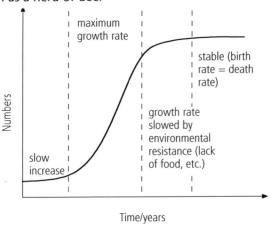

maximum growth rate

stable (birth rate = death rate)

growth rate slowed by environmental resistance (lack of food, etc.)

slow increase

Numbers

Time/years

Fig. 21.3 *Method of calculating rate of change. The method shows the rate of change in height at Day 7*

From the graph: $y = 33$ mm
$x = 5.6$ days

Therefore rate of growth $= \dfrac{1}{x} = \dfrac{33}{5.6}$

$= 5.9$ mm day^{-1}

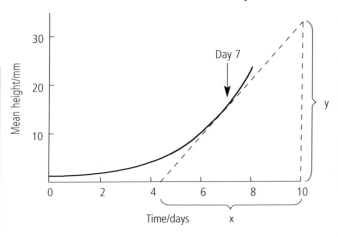

Mean height/mm

Day 7

Time/days x

Table 21.2 *Differences between nervous and endocrine coordination*

Nervous	Endocrine
Information passes along nerves as electrical impulses	Information passed as a chemical substance through the blood stream
Rapid transmission	Slow transmission
Response immediate	Response usually slow e.g. growth
Response short-lived	Response long-lasting
Response very exact by muscle or gland	Response usually widespread

21.1 Some terms

Growth – a gradual permanent increase in size (volume or mass) of an organism involving increase in cell number and/or size. True growth is best measured by determining the increase in dry mass of the organism.

Growth curve – a graphical representation of the growth rate of an organism; the growth rate varies throughout life and this can be shown by a growth curve. Growth can be measured in a variety of ways.

1 **Mass**

   (a) **Wet mass** is determined simply by weighing organisms at intervals throughout life e.g. dogs, cats, mice, rabbits or humans.

Fig. 21.4 *Growth curve of an herbaceous plant from seed to death*

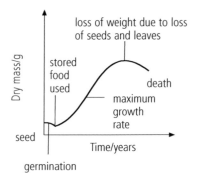

loss of weight due to loss of seeds and leaves

stored food used

death

maximum growth rate

Dry mass/g

seed

Time/years

germination

(b) **Dry mass** (when all water is removed) is more significant than wet mass but it cannot be used easily, except with plants. It measures the amount of *new* organic material and is best used for investigating growth of plants. In determining the dry mass of a selected plant species a large number of seeds are sown all at the same time. Once the seeds have germinated, batches of seedlings are selected at intervals (daily or every two or three days). These are dried in an oven at 110°C for 24 hours. At the end of the drying period the plant material is cooled in a dessicator, to prevent absorption of atmospheric water, and weighed to determine the mass. Heating, cooling and weighing are repeated until there is no further change in mass, i.e. until a constant mass has been attained. Using the final mass of each batch, a graph (growth curve) can be drawn. The dry mass is plotted on the vertical (Y) axis and time on the horizontal (X) axis. From the graph the pattern and extent of growth can be seen.

2 **Length** is a **single dimension**. It is easy to measure (e.g. height of child, tail length of mice, length of growing shoots). This method is imperfect because it disregards growth in other directions.

3 **Area** measures **two dimensions** (e.g. leaf surface area, by drawing an outline of the leaf on graph paper and then counting the squares, see Fig. 21.5). The calculation is as follows:
(numbered 1–6) cm^2 = 6 = 600 mm^2
(squares with dots) = 124 mm^2
(shaded squares) = 27 mm^2
Total = 751 mm^2 = 7.51 cm^2
This method can be repeated at intervals with the same leaf thus giving a steady measure of area increase over a period of time.

4 **Number**. The steady increase in the number of leaves of a plant, in the number of animals in a population or in the number of bacteria in a colony can be used as a measure of growth.

21.2 Growth of mammals

The change from 'young' to 'adult' occurs at puberty in mammals. In humans the following changes appear in **both males and females**:
- hair grows under armpits and in pubic region;
- height and weight increases (see Fig. 21.6);
- sex hormones are secreted;
- sexual attraction to the opposite sex begins.

Fig. 21.5 *Method of growth measurement by recording and measuring leaf area*

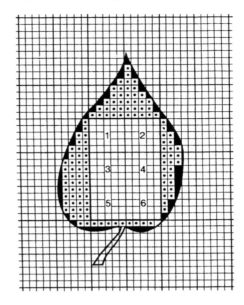

The following changes are specific to males or females:

Table 21.3 *Changes at puberty in males and females*

Males	Females
Voice deepens (larynx enlarges)	Breasts develop
Penis and scrotum enlarge	Uterus and vulva enlarge
Sperm production begins	Ovulation begins
Hair on face and chest grows	Menstruation begins

See Table 21.1 *Endocrine glands and their functions* for those hormones that affect human growth and development.

Fig. 21.6 *Growth curve for boys (solid line) and girls (broken line) showing the growth spurt during adolescence*

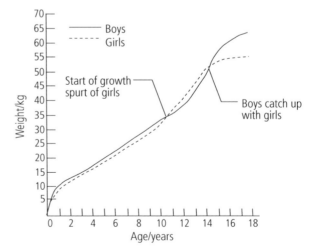

Note to students:
- Ensure that you can describe how growth is measured.
- Be able to draw and interpret growth curves.

22 Reproduction in humans

22.1 Some terms

Sexual reproduction – the production of new individuals by fertilisation, i.e. the fusion of male and female reproductive cells (gametes) to form a zygote, which divides by mitosis and gradually develops. Sexual reproduction usually involves the fusion of a small, motile gamete (**sperm**) with a large, non-motile female gamete (**ovum** or **egg cell**).

During the nuclear divisions preceding gamete formation, there is separation and recombination of chromosomes. This results in each gamete being genetically different. This mode of cell division is called **meiosis**. When the gametes fuse at fertilisation, a unique organism is produced. It has a different set of characteristics from both its parents and all other offspring produced by the same parents.

Offspring and parents are genetically different from each other.

Asexual reproduction – the production of new individuals without the formation of gametes. Asexual reproduction involves only one parent and all new cells are produced by mitosis so that the chromosome content of each new nucleus is always identical to that of the parent. Thus the offspring are identical to each other and to the parent; **they are clones**.

22.2 Sexual reproduction in humans

Humans may belong to either of two sexes (male or female), and reproduce sexually (see Figures 22.1 and 22.2 on p. 61 for the structure of the sex organs).

Female

Ova are formed in the **ovary**. Each **ovum** (Fig. 22.2(b)) develops within a group of **follicle cells**. When the ovum is mature it bursts through the surface of the ovary. The ovum (still surrounded by some follicle cells) is moved into the funnel of the **oviduct** by the action of **cilia** on the funnel.

The **uterus** is prepared for development of the fertilised ovum by the growth of a freshly formed lining. If fertilisation does not occur, the lining is then shed through the vagina, consisting of tissue and blood. This process is called **menstruation** or the monthly **period**. It occurs 12–14 days after the release of the ovum from the ovary.

Male

Spermatozoa (Fig. 22.1(b)) are formed in the **testes**. These are suspended outside of the body in a sac called the **scrotum**. Each testis contains a mass of **seminiferous tubules** in which the sperm are formed. The tubules join with a coiled tube at the edge of each testis (**epididymis**). Here sperm may be stored for a time. Each epididymis leads to a sperm duct (**vas deferens**) and the two ducts join the urethra that passes through the penis. To each sperm duct is attached a **seminal vesicle** and surrounding the junction of the sperm ducts is the **prostate** gland. Cowper's gland also discharges into the sperm duct at this point. These glands secrete the fluids in which the sperm swim.

Fig. 22.1 *(a) Reproductive organs of a man (b) Male gamete – sperm*

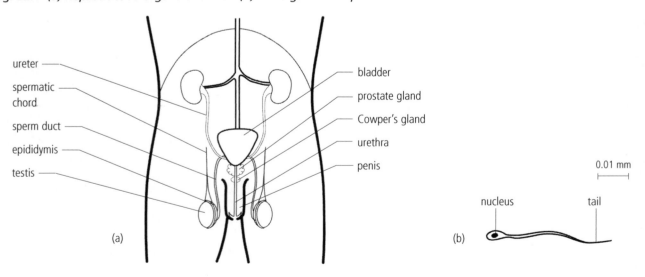

ureter

spermatic chord

sperm duct

epididymis

testis

bladder

prostate gland

Cowper's gland

urethra

penis

0.01 mm

nucleus   tail

(a)   (b)

Fig. 22.2 *(a) Reproductive organs of a woman – ventral view, arrow indicates the path of an ovum (b) Female gamete – egg*

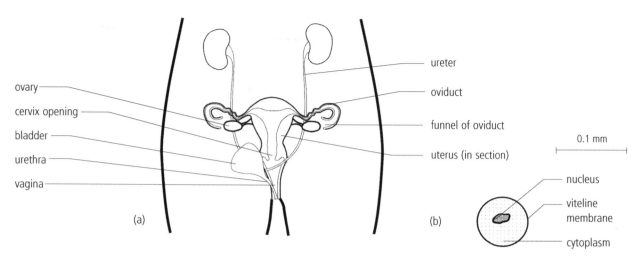

Fertilisation

Sexual arousal in males and females may lead to sexual intercourse or copulation. When sexual interest is aroused in the male, the penis becomes erect and stiff due to an increase in blood supply. In females the vagina becomes moist and muscles encasing the vagina relax. Under these conditions the penis can be inserted into the vagina. Movement in and out of the penis causes contraction of muscles at the base of the penis – ejaculation, which expels semen into the vagina. The sperm swim up through the uterus and into the oviduct. If there is an ovum moving down the oviduct at that time, it is penetrated (fertilised) by one sperm. All other sperm are prevented from entering. The zygote formed by fusion of sperm and ovum nuclei carries chromosomes from both the male and the female.

and one umbilical vein. The arteries take deoxygenated blood and metabolic waste from the foetus to the placenta while the vein takes oxygenated blood and nutrients from the placenta to the foetus. Thus **glucose, amino acids, salts** and **oxygen** pass across from mother to foetus. In the opposite direction **carbon dioxide** and **urea** pass out from foetus to mother. In addition, vitamins and antibodies pass from mother to foetus to protect it during growth. Prescription and non-prescription drugs can also cross the placenta, as well as some viruses.

The foetus is completely enclosed in a membrane called the **amnion** (water sac), which contains amniotic fluid to support the growing foetus. This fluid also protects the foetus from mechanical damage or shock as the mother moves.

Foetal development

The zygote divides rapidly by mitosis, forming a ball of cells (the blastocyst) and passes through the oviduct into the uterus. After four to five days it sinks into the prepared inner wall of the uterus (**implantation**). The blastocyst continues to grow and, at the same time, finger-like projections grow from the outer wall of the blastocyst (**villi**) into the lining of the uterus. These villi become part of the **placenta** (see Fig. 22.3). This is a disc of tissue on the inner wall of the uterus with large blood spaces in it and extensive capillary networks from both mother and foetus. The blood systems do not connect directly but the walls between them are very thin.

The umbilical cord takes foetal blood to and from the placenta. Within the cord are two umbilical arteries

Fig. 22.3 *Foetus in the womb showing its relationship with the uterus by way of the umbilical cord and placenta*

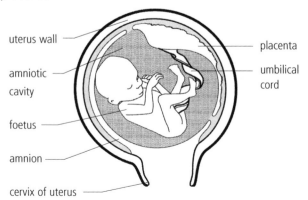

Pre-natal care

The pregnant woman should be cared for by health services (pre-natal clinics) during the period of pregnancy. The following are important aspects:

1 **weight measurement** – weight gain should be about 0.5 kg per week; excessive weight gain must be monitored as it may result from water retention; insufficient weight gain is also a danger sign;
2 **uterus size**;
3 **blood pressure**;
4 **blood tests** – these determine blood group and also are used for a haemoglobin count and HIV status;
5 **urine tests** – these check blood sugar levels and also albumen.

Other aspects of care:

1 **correct diet** – a balanced diet is needed, to ensure that all requirements for maternal health and growth of foetus are present;
2 **avoidance** of alcohol, smoking and other **drugs**;
3 **adequate rest** and **exercise**.

Birth and post-natal care

The developing human foetus is carried for 266 days, divided into three trimesters. The first involves active differentiation of the zygote, the second and third growth and development. At 36–40 weeks the head of the foetus becomes **engaged** above the **cervix**, ready for birth.

Birth begins with the contraction of the uterine muscles and the release of the amniotic fluid (water). Rhythmic contractions (**labour**) continue at shorter intervals and eventually the baby is expelled, usually head first. The time taken for birth can vary from one hour to one or two days. At birth the baby changes from being dependent on maternal oxygen supplied via the blood, to breathing air as the lungs begin to function.

The contractions of the uterus continue and the **placenta** and **umbilical cord (afterbirth)** are pushed out through the uterus and vagina. Within 24 hours a pituitary hormone (**prolactin**) stimulates the production of milk in the breasts. The first milk is a yellow-coloured fluid called **colostrum**, which is rich in vitamins and antibodies.

After a period of rest the mother can resume a modified routine in which she takes care of herself and her infant. Diet is still important to ensure an adequate and correctly balanced milk flow. In humans, parental care is very important since the young children have a long period of dependency on their parents. They need shelter, food and love, together with education and training.

23 Birth control

A major problem confronting the world is overpopulation. There are too many people and not enough food in some parts of the world to prevent starvation, malnutrition, spread of diseases and environmental degradation.

All methods used to regulate or prevent the birth of children are referred to as birth control, family planning, fertility control or planned parenthood.

Birth control: for and against

Some people support birth control:

- To limit the size of rapidly growing populations in some countries where resources may not be adequate. Governments of these countries may actively encourage couples to limit the size of their families.
- To manage the reproductive health of adolescents and so prevent teenage pregnancy and abandoned studies.
- To avoid unwanted pregnancies; to limit the number of children; or to space the birth of children to be able to provide the time and money required to raise a child well.
- To protect the mother's health if she is unwell, or to prevent the transmission of genetic disorders from one or both parents, e.g. if both partners are carriers of the sickle cell trait.

Other people oppose birth control:

- To discourage pre-marital sex and promiscuity.
- To protect their health and avoid the side-effects of chemical birth control.
- To protect their right to procreate and avoid the political control exerted by governments that impose birth control.
- To protect all life, even embyronic life, as a religious principle.

23.1 Methods of birth control

There are a number of ways in which the spacing of births can be carefully planned.

Contraceptives are devices used to **prevent conception or pregnancy**. Some are also useful in preventing sexually transmitted infections – STIs.

Avoiding sexual intercourse (**abstinence**) is 100% effective in preventing pregnancy and is also a means of preventing sexually transmitted diseases – STIs. It, however, requires self-discipline and control.

Physical or barrier methods

These involve some type of barrier that prevents the sperm reaching the egg. The **male condom** (or latex sheath) is a closed tube of thin rubber. It is purchased rolled up in sealed packets and is unrolled over the erect penis before intercourse. After ejaculation, the semen collects in a small pocket at the end of the condom (see Fig. 23.1(a)).

The **female condom** is made up of plastic tubing fitted inside the vagina before sex to cover the cervix and vagina. It is secured externally (see Fig. 23.1 (b)).

Both male and female condoms are about 85% effective in preventing pregnancy and both reduce the risk of contracting STIs.

Fig. 23.1 *Barrier methods of contraception (a) Male condom (b) Female condom (c) Intrauterine device: prevents implantation of embryo*

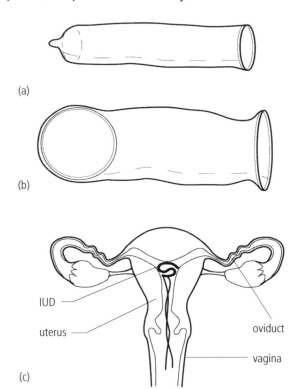

(a)

(b)

IUD

uterus

oviduct

vagina

(c)

The **intrauterine contraceptive** device (IUCD or IUD for short) is made of plastic and metal. It is positioned within the uterus by a doctor or trained family planning health worker. Its function is to prevent the fertilised egg becoming implanted in uterine wall and it is more than 90% effective (see Fig. 23.1 (c)).

Fig. 23.2 *Diaphragm: a barrier method of*

contraception

The **diaphragm or cervical cap** is a rubber dome that

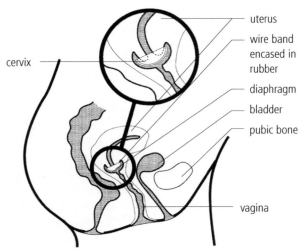

fits over the cervix of the uterus at the upper end of the vagina and must be inserted before sex. The cap is smaller than the diaphragm. It is generally used in conjunction with a **spermicidal cream** to increase effectiveness. It prevents sperm from reaching the opening of the uterus. Like the condom it is about 85% effective in preventing pregnancy (see Fig. 23.2).

Chemical methods

Spermicidal jellies, creams, foams, pessaries are placed into the vagina and are capable of killing sperm released during intercourse. They are about 75% effective and even more efficient if used in conjunction with a barrier method.

The **oral contraceptive pill** is taken by mouth. The pill contains a mixture of **oestrogen** and **progesterone-like hormones**. These act by preventing ovulation. Females must take the pill every day or as directed by a health professional. This is an extremely efficient method (90–100%). There are side-effects, so the pill is taken only after consultation with a doctor or other health practitioner.

Natural or rhythm method

The natural method restricts sexual intercourse to the 'safe period' (before and after ovulation). Ovulation normally occurs some 12–14 days after the end of the menstruation and can be more exactly determined by taking daily temperature readings and monitoring daily

the viscosity of vaginal secretions. This is based on the fact that the body temperature rises by about 1°C at the time of ovulation and secretions also change in texture throughout the cycle. This is the least reliable method of birth control – 70% – since the menstrual cycle can vary in length. It is also now suggested that some women may ovulate twice per cycle, making it more risky to utilise this method. Certain religious authorities support this method since it uses no artificial methods of preventing conception.

Fig 23.3 *Rhythm method of contraception showing the two safe periods during a menstrual cycle*

Sterilisation

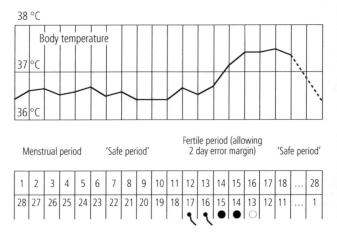

- ● Probable ovulation

- ○ Possible egg survival

- ↙ Possible sperm survival after intercourse on day 11

This method involves the cutting or sealing of tubes through which the gametes pass. **Tubal ligation** in females involves removal of a piece of oviduct under general anaesthetic in hospital (Fig. 23.4 on p. 65). In males, under local anaesthetic, the doctor cuts and ties the sperm ducts (**vasectomy**) (Fig. 23.5 on p. 65). The male operation can, with proper arrangements, be performed in a way that makes it reversible. The female operation is not reversible and therefore must be carefully considered particularly by young people who might wish to have a child at a later date.

Fig. 23.4 *Sterilisation of a female by cutting of the*

oviducts   sperm ducts (vasectomy)
Fig. 23.5 *Sterilisation of a male by cutting of the*

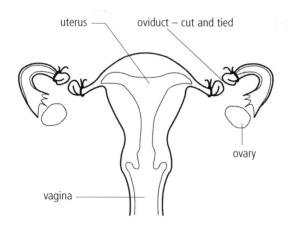

uterus —   oviduct – cut and tied

ovary

vagina —

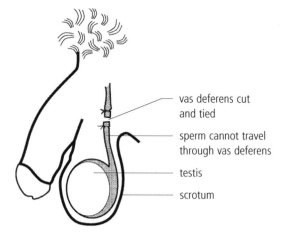

vas deferens cut
and tied

sperm cannot travel
through vas deferens

testis

scrotum

24 Cell division

Cell division involves first the division of the nucleus followed by the division of cytoplasm and all organelles. There are two processes by which the nucleus divides, namely, **mitosis** and **meiosis**

24.1 Mitosis

This process of nuclear division results in the formation of two daughter nuclei from a single parent nucleus. Each is genetically identical to the other and the parent nucleus. Each has the same number of chromosomes (referred to as the diploid number '2n') and same arrangement of DNA.

Mitosis is important for growth processes, leading to an increase in cell number.

In asexual reproduction, mitosis is the mechanism that produces genetially identical offspring – organisms or cells called **clones**. It is common in unicellular organisms such as bacteria, yeast and amoeba. When it occurs in plants, it is known as vegetative propagation, e.g. the use of stem cuttings to propagate sugar cane. The cuttings consist of several nodes or 'joints', where buds consisting of unspecialised cells divide to form leaves, roots and ultimately entirely new plants. *Bryophyllum* leaves also produce tiny plantlets along leaf margins. Each can grow independently into a new plant under favourable conditions.

Fig. 24.1 *A leaf of Bryophyllum showing vegetative reproduction of young plants at the leaf margins*

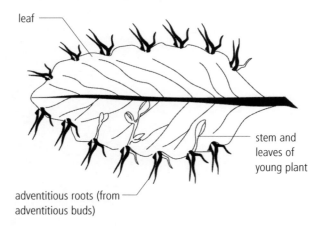

The process of mitosis

At the beginning of mitosis the chromosomes shorten and thicken, becoming more visible. Each chromosome consists of two **chromatids held together by a centromere**.

Fig. 24.2

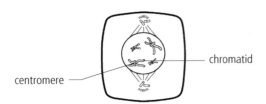

The **nuclear membrane** breaks down. The **fibrils** of the **spindle** appear. Chromosomes become attached to the spindle at the centromeres.

Fig. 24.3

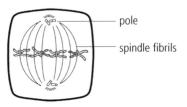

Chromatids separate and are moved to opposite poles of the dividing cell by contraction of the spindle fibres.

Fig. 24.4

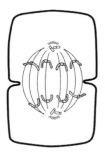

Each chromatid at each pole replicates, forming a new chromosome. The **cytoplasm** divides, new nuclear membranes form around each set of chromosomes and the nucleolus reappears.

Fig. 24.5

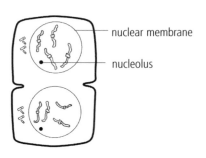

24.2 Meiosis

This process of nuclear division results in the formation of four daughter nuclei from a single parent nucleus. Each is genetically different from the other and from the parent nucleus. Each has half the number of chromosomes (the haploid number 'n') in the parent nucleus and the DNA may also be different. Meiosis is the basis of sexual reproduction. This is the process by which gametes are formed.

The process of meiosis

First meiotic division

The chromosomes shorten and thicken, becoming more visible and combining in matching pairs (homologous chromosomes).

Fig. 24.6

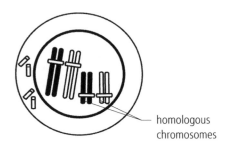

homologous chromosomes

The nuclear membrane disappears. Each chromosome has divided into two chromatids, so a pair of homologous chromosomes is now called a **bivalent**. Each chromosome becomes attached to the spindle at the centromere. The fibrils of the spindle contract and separate into homologous chromosomes. As a result of the entanglement of chromatids at separation, portions are exchanged (crossing-over).

Fig. 24.7

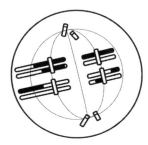

One of each pair of chromosomes (half of a bivalent) moves to each pole, thus halving the number of chromosomes in the new nuclei. The **cytoplasm**

divides and a nuclear membrane forms around each set of chromosomes. At the end of the first meiotic division two new daughter cells are formed. Each enters the second meiotic division.

Fig. 24.8

Second meiotic division

Chromosomes still consist of chromatids joined together at the centromere. These line up on the equator of the spindle, attaching to it with their centromeres. Contraction of the spindle fibres split the centromeres so that chromatids are drawn to opposite poles of the cell.

Fig. 24.9

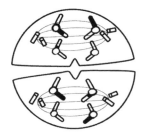

Four nuclei are formed and each chromatid replicates becoming a chromosome; the **cytoplasm** divides and new nuclear membranes form around each set of chromosomes. Thus each new nucleus has half of the original number of chromosomes (i.e. it is haploid).

Fig. 24.10

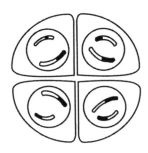

Table 24.1 *Comparison of mitosis and meiosis*

Mitosis	Meiosis
Occurs during growth of embryo and body cells (e.g. at growing points of root and stem)	Occurs during production of gametes
The chromosome number in nuclei of body cells (2n) and of new cells (2n) is the same	The chromosome number in nuclei of new cells is half (n) the number of cells of the parent cells (2n)
From each dividing nucleus (diploid, 2n) two new diploid cells are produced	From each dividing diploid nucleus four nuclei (haploid, n) are produced
Each chromosome has two chromatids connected by a centro-mere in the nuclei of parents cells and in the new cells (homologous chromosomes)	The parent cell has homologous chromosomes in its nucleus but new nuclei have only one of each pair of chromosomes
No exchange of material between chromatids occurs	There is an exchange of material between chromatids (crossing over) of homologous chromosomes in nucleus. This results in genetic variation of offspring.

24.3 Gametes and fertilisation

Any one species has a constant number of chromosomes in the nuclei of the body cells, e.g. human cells have 46 (**diploid number = 2n**). Sexual reproduction involves fusion of the nuclei of male and female gametes. If the number of chromosomes in gamete nuclei were the same as the number in body cell nuclei, then at every fertilisation the chromosome number would double.

As a result of meiosis during gamete formation, the number of chromosomes in each nucleus is halved (**haploid number = n**), i.e. 23 for humans. Thus fusion of two haploid gametes restores the original diploid number.

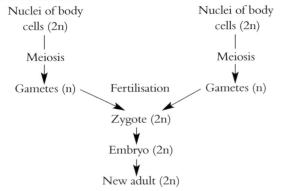

As a result of the halving the chromosome number in producing each gamete nucleus, at fertilisation the zygote receives half of its chromosomes from one parent and half from the other. This means that the offspring can show variation, i.e., differences in characteristics between individuals of the same species. These genetic variations (nature) give each individual a potential to develop, given a favourable environment. The influence of the environment (nurture) can cause variation between organisms. A summary of this relationship is:

Genetic composition = genotype
Genotype + factors in the environment = **Phenotype**

Do remember that environmental factors can be biotic and abiotic.

25 Genetics

25.1 Some terms

Gene – a segment of a DNA molecule on a chromosome coding for a protein such as the enzyme that catalyses the formation of melanin.

Melanin is the pigment found in the skin. The major role of melanin in the skin is to absorb the ultraviolet light that comes from the sun to protect the skin from damage. All people have about the same number of **melanocytes** – melanin-producing cells. Those of dark-skinned people produce more melanin than those of light-skinned people. Exposure to sunlight increases the production of melanin, causing light skin to tan and dark skin becomes darker.

Allele – different forms of the same gene that occupy the same position or **locus** on homologous chromosomes. Only one can occur at a locus. Each form of the gene exhibits different characteristics. Thus there can be one form of the gene coding for the enzyme that catalyses melanin formation and another that codes for a defective enzyme.

Genotype – genetic make up of an organism with respect to specific alleles. The genotype may be homozygous or heterozygous.

Homozygous – cell or organism in which alleles at a specific locus on homologous chromosomes are the same. Thus an individual can have in their cells two alleles for a functional enzyme or two for a defective enzyme.

Heterozygous – cell or organism in which alleles at a specific locus on homologous chromosomes are different. Thus an individual can have in their cells one allele for a functional enzyme and another for a non-functional enzyme.

Phenotype – characteristics of an organism due to the effect of the environment on the genotype. Melanocytes that have the alleles for a functional enzyme can make melanin. Exposure to sunlight, as previously noted, increases the production of melanin.

Dominant – the allele that shows its effect in the **phenotype**, even in the presence of a different allele. A dominant allele codes for the enzyme catalysing the production of melanin. Individuals who have normally pigmented skin are either heterozygous or homozygous dominant for the dominant allele.

Recessive – the allele that has no effect in the phenotype in the presence of another, different allele. It is expressed only when there are two identical alleles present. A recessive allele codes for the defective enzyme catalysing the production of melanin. Individuals who have two recessive alleles (homozygous recessive) are albinos. They have milky-white skin, white hair, and pink eyes. Their skin does not tan with exposure to the sun and is sensitive to the sunlight so that they develop sunburn.

Codominance occurs when two different alleles of the same gene are both expressed in the phenotype of a heterozygote. For example, assuming the gene for flower colour in a particular plant species has two alleles, and there are three phenotypes: red, white and pink flowers. Both red and white flowers would have homozygous genotypes and pink flowers would be heterozygous. In this case, the alleles for red and white flower colour are said to be codominant.

25.2 Genetic diagrams

The inheritance of genetic characteristics can be summarised using genetic diagrams that have a standard format. To construct a genetic diagram we usually:

1 Choose a single letter to represent the alleles of the gene controlling the characteristic – usually the first letter of the trait, e.g. albinism 'A'. When selecting an appropriate letter it is best to choose one in which the upper and lower case forms of the letter differ in shape and size. The upper case must always be written in front of the lower case letter.
2 State clearly what each letter represents.
3 Circle gametes.
4 Possible combinations due to random fertilisation are demonstrated using a Punnet square or diamond.

Assume two individuals with normal skin pigmentation but a heterozygous genotype for the alleles. A genetic diagram to show the inheritance of this characteristic can be constructed as follows.

Let **A** represent the normal allele for the enzyme catalysing the formation of melanin and **a** represent the recessive allele for the enzyme if lacking or defective so there is no formation of melanin:

Parental	Phenotype	Normal pigment	×	Normal pigment
Parental	Genotype	**Aa**	×	**Aa**

Note that both parents are 'carriers', that is they possess the recessive allele for albinism.

Gametes

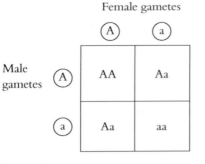

Female gametes

	A	a
Male gametes A	AA	Aa
a	Aa	aa

Offspring   Genotype   **AA**   **Aa**   **Aa**   **aa**

Offspring   Phenotype 3 normal   1 albino

Albinos can of course reach adulthood and produce children. Possible crosses are:

1   Albino × normal (homozygous)
    All offspring are normal (carriers) or
2   Albino × normal (heterozygote)
    $\frac{1}{2}$ albino and $\frac{1}{2}$ normal (heterozygote) offspring

Codominant alleles

In representing codominant alleles, a capital letter is used to represent the gene for the trait being discussed and a capital letter superscript for the allele.
Let C^R represent the allele for red flower colour and C^W the allele for white flower colour.

Parental Phenotype   red flower   ×   white flower
Parental Genotype $C^R C^R$ × $C^W C^W$
Gametes C^R C^R C^W C^W

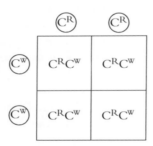

	C^R	C^R
C^W	$C^R C^W$	$C^R C^W$
C^W	$C^R C^W$	$C^R C^W$

F_1 Genotype   All $C^R C^W$
F_1 Phenotype   All pink flowers

If the F1 plants are self-fertilised, then
Parental phenotype   pink flowers   ×   pink flowers
Parental genotype $C^R C^W$ × $C^R C^W$
Gametes C^R C^W C^R C^W

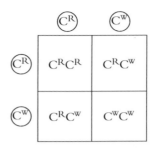

	C^R	C^W
C^R	$C^R C^R$	$C^R C^W$
C^W	$C^R C^W$	$C^W C^W$

F_2 Genotype $C^R C^R$ $C^R C^W$ $C^R C^W$ $C^W C^W$
F_2 Phenotype   red flowers pink flowers pink flowers white flowers
Ratio of F2 phenotypes   1 red: 2 pink: 1 white

The term F1 applies to offspring resulting from crossing parents who are both homozygous – have two identical alleles. The term F2 applies to offspring resulting from crossing F1 parents – heterozygotes each having two different alleles. In all other cases, the term offspring is used.

Blood groups

Inheritance of blood groups is determined by three alleles I^A, I^B and I^O. Both I^A and I^B are dominant to I^O, but I^A is not dominant to I^B nor is I^B to I^A. Thus I^A to I^B are said to be codominant. The different blood groups have the following genotypes and phenotypes.

Blood group A – Genotype $I^A I^A$ $I^A I^O$
                              homozygous   heterozygous
Blood group B – Genotype $I^B I^B$ $I^B I^O$
                              homozygous   heterozygous
Blood group AB – Genotype $I^A I^B$
                              heterozygous
Blood group O – Genotype $I^O I^O$
                              homozygous

An example of inheritance of blood groups is given below:

Parental Phenotype   Man   ×   Woman
                          Group A   Group AB
Parental Genotype $I^A I^O$ × $I^A I^B$

Gametes I^A I^O I^A I^B

Female gametes

	I^A	I^B
Male gametes I^A	$I^A I^A$	$I^A I^B$
I^O	$I^A I^O$	$I^B I^O$

Offspring genotype
Offspring phenotype
(blood group)

Sickle cell anaemia

In sickle cell anaemia the normal haemoglobin in the red cell is replaced by abnormal haemoglobin called haemoglobin S. This abnormal haemoglobin is produced by a faulty allele. The red blood cells assume a crescent or sickle shape when oxygen concentrations are low.

Normal haemoglobin – genotype Hb^AHb^A (homozygous).

Sickle cell anaemia – genotype Hb^SHb^S (homozygous – 'sickle cell disease'). This condition is debilitating and can be fatal if not well managed.

Sickle cell trait – genotype Hb^AHb^S (heterozygous – 'carriers'). In individuals suffering from the sickle cell trait, only about 50% of the red blood cells are altered and the remainder are of a normal shape. The result is only a slight anaemia.

An example of inheritance of sickle cell anaemia is given below:

Parental	Phenotype	Male carrier	×	Female carrier
Parental	Genotype	Hb^AHb^S	×	Hb^AHb^S

Gametes Hb^A Hb^S Hb^A Hb^S

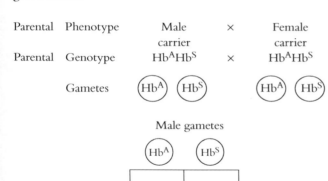

	Offspring			
Genotype	Hb^AHb^A	Hb^AHb^S	Hb^AHb^S	Hb^SHb^S
Offspring Phenotype	normal	carrier	carrier	'sickle cell disease'

We see, therefore, that carriers have a one in four chance of producing a child with sickle cell disease.

Sex determination

Humans have 46 chromosomes in the nuclei of their cells (2n = 46). In females there are 22 pairs + XX and in males 22 pairs + XY. The pairs of chromosomes denoted as XX and XY are called the sex chromosomes. During meiosis and gamete formation they separate with one chromosome in each gamete. Thus:

Parental Phenotype	Male	×	Female
Genotype	XY	×	XX

Gametes (X) (Y)   (X) (X)

Male gametes

	(X)	(Y)
Female gametes (X)	XX	XY
(X)	XX	XY

Offspring Genotype	XX	XX	XY	XY
Offspring Phenotype	½ female		½ male	

Note that in writing the genotype of the male, the X is always written before the Y. Certain genes are found on the X chromosome; these are sex-linked genes. A recessive allele on the X chromosome of a mother, that is passed on to her son will be evident in the phenotype because there is no allele on the Y chromosome to mask it.

Haemophilia is a condition in which a blood clotting protein – human factor VIII – is missing. This is due to a faulty gene on the X chromosome. When untreated, affected individuals bleed to death. Consider the outcome if a female carrier of the allele produced offspring with a normal male.

Note that in genetic crosses involving sex-linked genes the dominant or recessive alleles of the gene are written as upper and lower case superscripts on the specific sex chromosomes. Thus:

Let X^h – X chromosome carrying the allele for haemophilia
and X^H – X chromosome carrying the normal allele

Parental Phenotype	Female carrier	Normal male
Parental Genotype	X^HX^h	X^HY

Gametes (X^H) (X^h)   (X^H) (Y)

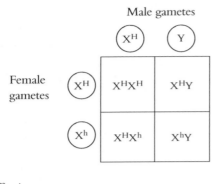

Male gametes

Female gametes

	X^H	Y
X^H	$X^H X^H$	$X^H Y$
X^h	$X^H X^h$	$X^h Y$

Offspring genotypes	$X^H X^H$	$X^H X^h$	$X^H Y$	$X^h Y$
Offspring phenotypes	Normal female	Carrier female	Normal male	Male haemophiliac

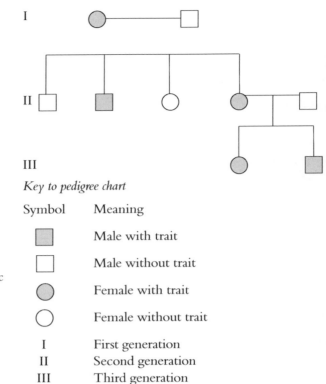

Key to pedigree chart

Symbol	Meaning
■ (grey square)	Male with trait
□	Male without trait
● (grey circle)	Female with trait
○	Female without trait
I	First generation
II	Second generation
III	Third generation

25.3 Pedigree charts

Pedigree charts show the pattern of inheritance for a particular genetic condition. If the pattern of inheritance is known and the genotype of the parents, the chances of inheriting the condition can be predicted.

- A line between a square and circle indicates a union.
- A downward vertical line indicates a child or offspring of the union.
- A horizontal line perpendicular to a downward vertical line indicates several children.
- Males and females with a specific trait may be homozygous or heterozygous.
- Other symbols used in the construction of a pedigree chart are shown in the key.

26 Variation and selection

[syllabus sections C2.6; C4.1 to 5.2]

26.1 Variation

Variation is defined as the phenotypic differences between individuals within a species. It is due to the effects of the genotype and/or the environment.

Examples of variation include:

1 Variation of races within the human species (*Homo sapiens*); as evidenced by differences in eye colour and shape, skin colour, hair colour and texture, body size and shape.
2 Variation of dog breeds all derived from a single species of wild dog. All domestic dogs belong to a single species (*Canis familaris*). Different breeds have been produced for hunting deer, herding sheep, guarding skills and guiding the blind.
3 Variation in the flowers of *Hibiscus* plants – they may be of different colours or shapes, single (one whorl of petals) or double (several whorls of petals). Horticulturists have bred all of them.

Phenotypic variation is of two types – discontinuous and continuous.

Discontinuous variation

This refers to clearly defined differences within a population, for example:

1 **Tongue rolling** – Some people cannot control their tongue muscles to roll their tongue but most can roll it from each side to the mid-line. Tongue rolling is controlled by a dominant allele.
2 **'Free' ear lobes** – in humans the earlobe may hang freely or be attached directly to the side of the head. Individuals with attached earlobes are either homozygous dominant or heterozygous for the allele. Those with 'free' earlobes are homozygous recessive for the allele.
3 The **four major human blood groups** (A, B, AB and O) are another example of this type of variation. There is no in-between group as each is quite distinctive and separate.
4 **Polled** – is the term used to refer to the absence of horns, which is characteristic of some breeds of cattle such as Holsteins and the Jamaica Red Poll. Polled animals have a dominant allele while horned animals do not.

Discontinuous variation is genetically determined, often controlled by a single gene, and not influenced by environmental conditions.

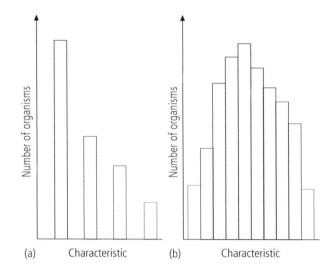

Fig. 26.1 *Histograms representing frequency distribution of (a) discontinuous variation and (b) continuous variation*

Continuous variation

Certain characteristics show a range of forms in any given population. People, for example, are neither tall nor short (as in pea plants) but there is a whole range of intermediate heights from very tall to very short. These are still genetically determined but they are under the influence of several genes.

Continuous variation is genetically determined, and more likely to be influenced by environmental conditions. Individuals do not reach their full height potential if they are undernourished in the early years of growth.

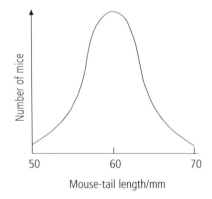

Fig. 26.2 *Graph showing distribution of tail length in a population of mice i.e. continuous variation*

Traits or characteristics showing continuous variation can be measured, e.g. length of leaves, length of mouse-tails, plant height, weight of a population of animals.

Typically, most of the individuals in any study fall near the middle of the range with fewer individuals at the two extremes (see Fig. 26.2).

26.2 Natural selection

Organisms vary genetically from each other. Because of this genetic variation some organisms are better adapted to a given environment and so have a greater chance of surviving, finding a mate, reproducing and so passing their favourable genes on to their offspring.

Natural selection can lead to a change in the characteristics of organism, as, for example, in **industrial melanism**. In an industrial area of England in 1848 a black variety of a normally light coloured moth, the peppered moth (*Biston betularia*) was identified. By 1895 the numbers had increased to 98% of the population in that particular district. The light-coloured forms were usually well camouflaged against the lichens on the tree trunks where they rested.

Atmospheric pollution in the industrial areas reduced the lichens and darkened the tree trunks with soot. On the dark coloured trunks the dark moths were better concealed than the light forms. The light forms were preyed upon and eaten by birds because they were now easily identified.

This is an example of natural selection in action. The change in the environmental conditions due to atmospheric pollution favoured the black variety, which was able to reproduce successfully. The light-coloured variety was preyed upon and so unable to reproduce.

In many cases the dark coloured forms had a single dominant allele in their genotype coding for this specific colour.

Charles Darwin proposed that natural selection was the mechanism by which new species arise from existing species. It is based on **competition between individuals** so that animals and plants possessing **variations that are advantageous** are **better able to survive**. For instance, stronger, faster animals might be able to obtain food at the expense of weaker ones. The result will be that in successive generations, those possessing these favourable characteristics will be in a better position to breed and thereby pass on these traits to their offspring. Similarly, in plants, the fastest growing ones will compete more successfully for light and air than those that grow slowly.

26.3 Artificial selection

Humans have selected animals and plants to breed for domestic use since early civilisation. Darwin based some of his evidence for natural selection on this practice. The basis is to **select** and **isolate** for **breeding purposes**, from natural populations, such organisms showing

characteristics **useful** to humans (e.g. sheep for their wool, cattle for their milk or meat yield, horses for their speed or endurance, sugar cane for increased sugar yield, banana for sweetness) (see Fig. 26.3).

Fig. 26.3 *Change in weight in two mouse populations in successive generations undergoing selection for body weight, i.e. artificial selection by humans*

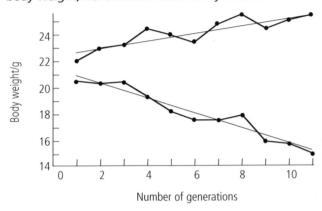

Techniques of artificial selection include:
1 **Inbreeding** between closely related organisms (e.g. offspring from the same parents) is often used to keep and increase particular characteristics, e.g. in chickens, to increase egg production.
2 **Outbreeding** (used in plant breeding particularly) involves crossing individuals from genetically distinct populations. The offspring are called **hybrids** and tend to be stronger and more adaptable than the parental types (e.g. in corn, where hybridisation has doubled the grain yield).

Genetic engineering

Genetic engineering involves changing the characteristics of organisms by inserting genes from other organisms into its DNA. Supporters of genetic engineering suggest that it is necessary in order to provide food to match population growth and to treat debilitating genetic disorders, and to diagnose and treat other forms of disease.

Crops such as cotton, wheat, soybean, canola, sugar beet, potatoes and tomatoes have been genetically engineered and are termed GM crops. The objectives of genetically modifying crops include:
1 Improved food quality – A strain of 'golden' rice containing an unusually high content of beta-carotene (vitamin A) has been developed to counteract blindness due to vitamin A deficiency.
2 Resistance of crop plants to pests, diseases, environmental conditions and herbicides.
 (a) Bacterium genes inserted into corn enables the corn to produce its own pesticides against

insects such as the European corn borer. The plant produces proteins that are lethal to borer larvae.

(b) There are many viruses, fungi and bacteria that cause plant diseases, reducing quality and yield. Plant biologists are working to create plants with genetically engineered resistance to these diseases.

(c) Crop plants are genetically engineered to be resistant to one very powerful herbicide, which could help prevent environmental damage by reducing the amount of herbicides needed.

(d) Crop plants can be made tolerant to drought, heat, and wind damage, acidic, saline or waterlogged soils. Crops modified to grow in adverse conditions can boost production in such areas.

3 Medical applications include:

(a) Making human growth hormone to treat dwarfism

(b) Human insulin production for diabetics

(c) Human factor VIII – an important clotting factor for haemophiliacs

(d) Vaccines

(e) Cancer diagnosis and treatment

(f) Diagnosis of genetic disorders

(g) Curing genetic disorders.

Criticisms of genetic engineering

1 **Social and ethical** – There is not adequate scientific understanding of the impact on human health and GM products may cause allergic reactions. Extensive testing of genetically manufactured (GM) foods may be required to avoid the possibility of harm to consumers with food allergies. The price of seeds may become so high that small farmers and developing countries will not be able to afford seeds for GM crops, thus widening the gap between the wealthy and the poor.

2 **Religious** – Some viewpoints suggest that humans may be 'playing God'.

3 **Ecological** – There is not adequate scientific understanding of the impact of GM products on the environment. Suggested adverse effects include:

(a) Genetically engineered (GE) organisms can reproduce and interbreed with natural organisms, thereby spreading to new environments and future generations in an unpredictable and uncontrollable way, possibly causing loss of genetic variation.

(b) GM crops cross-pollinating with each other to produce strains resistant to more than one herbicide could create crops that behave like super-weeds in time.

Because of several concerns, some countries, many in Europe, have imposed bans on importing and growing GM crops. Measures such as labelling of genetically engineered ingredients, and the segregation of genetically engineered crops from conventional ones are recommended by organisations such as Greenpeace. Education of consumers is important so that they can choose whether or not they are willing to use these products in spite of the uncertain risks.

27 Disease and drug abuse

[syllabus sections D1.1 to 1.2; 2.1 to 2.6; 3.2]

Diseases can be grouped into four categories **pathogenic**, **deficiency**, **physiological** and **hereditary**.

27.1 Pathogenic diseases

Pathogenic diseases are also referred to as infectious or communicable and are caused by **pathogenic organisms**, which include viruses, bacteria, fungi, protozoans, worms and insects.

Table 27.1 *Pathogens that may affect crops*

Disease name	Causative organism	Crop affected
Bunchy top	Virus	Banana
Panama disease	Fungus	Banana
Moko	Bacterium	Banana
Red rot	Fungus	Sugar cane
Smut	Fungus	Sugar cane
Lethal yellowing	Mycoplasma	Coconut
Tristeza	Virus	Citrus species

The role of vectors in the transmission of pathogenic disease

Some insects are vectors of organisms causing disease. Houseflies can carry virus particles on their feet, mouthparts and faeces; and bacteria, eggs of parasites from contaminated faeces to food (e.g. gastroenteritis and cholera). Mosquitoes carry pathogens inside their bodies, transmitting them by biting their hosts (e.g. malaria and dengue fever).

In attempting to control insect vectors the following must be considered:
- Where does the vector breed?
- Where does it rest?
- Is it cheaper to kill larvae or adults?

Control of pathogenic diseases

- If there is a vector – control the vector, especially at vulnerable stages in its lifecycle – egg, larval or pupal. Eliminate breeding sites.
- If there is an alternative host – treat host or eliminate where necessary.
- If there are infected individuals treat these; identify and treat carriers.
- If transmitted by contaminated food or water – ensure proper sanitation, especially the disposal of human faeces and hygienic food handling – wash hands after using the bathroom and before preparing food.

Table 27.2 *Examples of pathogenic diseases*

Disease	Causative organism	Method of transmission
Common cold	Virus	Droplet
Measles	Virus	Droplet
Chicken pox	Virus	Droplet
AIDS – Acquired Immune Deficiency Syndrome	Virus	Sexual contact; intravenous drug use; blood transfusion
Genital herpes	Virus	Sexual contact; mother to foetus in pregnancy
Dengue fever	Virus	*Aedes aegypti* mosquito vector
TB – Tuberculosis	Bacterium	Droplet; drinking milk from infected cattle
Gonorrhoea	Bacterium	Sexual contact; from mother to baby during delivery
Syphilis	Bacterium	Sexual contact; from mother to foetus during pregnancy
Cholera	Bacterium	Contamination of food, water, utensils by faeces
Gastroenteritis	Bacterium	Contamination of food, water, utensils by faeces
Food poisoning	Bacterium – *Salmonella*	Contamination of food, water, utensils by faeces
Malaria	Protozoan	*Anopheles* mosquito vector
Trichomoniasis – 'Trich'	Protozoan	Sexual contact

Droplet – water droplets in air produced during sneezing, coughing or talking.

Carriers – individuals who transmit a disease but show no symptoms themselves. They are difficult to identify, can transmit disease to others and also serve as a source of pathogens.

Vector – an intermediate organism that transmits pathogens from an infected human to an uninfected human, or from an infected animal to an uninfected human.

Stage of life cycle	Mosquito	Housefly
Adult	Use chemical sprays on resting areas; insect repellents; eliminate breeding sites; wear long-sleeved shirts; sleep under mosquito nets; install screens on doors and windows	Use chemical sprays; cover food; remove and bury or burn garbage daily
Egg	Empty standing water in old tyres, potted plants; cover stored water with mesh	Remove, bury or burn garbage daily

Fig. 27.1 Life cycle of mosquito

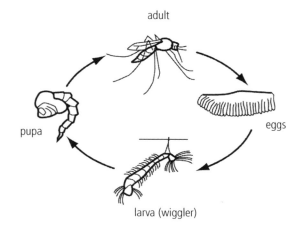

Fig. 27.2 *Life cycle of housefly*

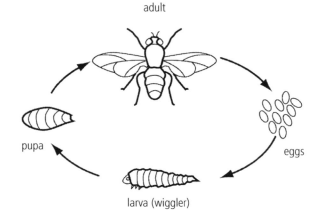

Role of blood in defending body against pathogenic disease

1. Blood clotting protects against the entry of bacteria

If blood vessels on the skin surface are damaged as the result of a wound, platelets release **thrombokinase** (an enzyme), which changes **prothrombin** in blood to **thrombin**. Thrombin converts **fibrinogen**, a soluble plasma protein, into long fibres of **fibrin**, an insoluble protein, which form a mesh over the wound. Blood cells become entangled forming a blood clot that dries to form a scab. Calcium is very important for this process. Clotting prevents further blood loss and the entry of bacteria.

2. Immunity is the body's protection against pathogenic disease

It involves the activity of:
- white blood cells (phagocytes) that engulf and digest bacteria; and
- lymphocytes that release **antibodies** to neutralise bacterial protein molecules (**antigens**).

Some antibodies neutralise **toxins** (poisons) produced by bacteria. Once these antibodies are produced they persist in the blood and provide protection against future infections by the same pathogens. Thus the body has immunity against further attack; this is called **acquired natural immunity**. Some people gain natural immunity against certain diseases without ever suffering from the symptoms.

Embryos in the uterus obtain **passive natural immunity** when antibodies cross the placenta from the maternal blood and enter foetal blood and when they drink mother's milk after birth.

3. Artificial protection by vaccination

A **vaccine** consists of antigens that will stimulate antibody production. It is introduced into the body orally or by injection, but it does not actually cause the disease symptoms. Several types of vaccine can be used:
- **weakened** pathogens (attenuated) by culturing outside the body, e.g. BCG given for TB;
- **killed** pathogens, e.g. typhoid;
- **extracts** of bacterial **toxins**, e.g. tetanus; or
- **genetically engineered**, e.g. Hepatitis B vaccine.

Use of such vaccines gives *artificial active immunity*. Another method is to inject antibodies produced by another human or an animal into the body. Small quantities of **serum** taken from a horse (which has been given **appropriate** antigens) are injected into the

Table 27.4 *Summary of types of immunity*

Active immunity (antibodies produced by patient's lymphocytes)	Passive immunity (antibodies produced by another animal)
Natural	
As a result of disease	Received from mother via placenta
Inherited	Received from mother via colostrum
Artificial	
From vaccination	From serum containing antibodies

blood. This is a short-term protection since the antibodies are gradually eliminated. This method is called **artificial passive immunity**.

Sexually transmitted infections (STIs)

These are pathogenic diseases spread by sexual contact from an infected to an uninfected individual.

Control of sexually transmitted infections is by:
- **Public education** so that individuals are able to identify the symptoms of STIs and are aware of the behaviour that increases their chances of becoming infected.
- **Abstinence**, i.e. no sexual intercourse.
- Sexual intercourse with **one faithful partner** who has been **tested** and is **known to be uninfected**.
- A **latex condom used** correctly and **every time**, although this is not 100% protection against the human papilloma virus, certain strains of which have now been linked to cervical cancer.
- **Identification**, **testing** and **treatment**, where necessary, of **sex partners**.

Treatment of sexually transmitted infections:
- **AIDS** – there is no cure; the use of antiretroviral drugs suppresses HIV but cannot eliminate it from the body. HIV positive individuals can live longer, but there are medical complications involved in the use of these drugs.
- **Syphilis** – can be cured if identified and treated early using penicillin injections or another doctor-prescribed antibiotic.
- **Gonorrhoea** – can be treated, but an individual can contract the disease again through sexual contact with an infected person. Treat with doctor-prescribed antibiotic.
- **Genital herpes** – no treatment to cure, antiviral medications to prevent and shorten outbreaks.
- **Trichomoniasis** – treated with a prescription drug called metronidazole.

Individuals who have had syphilis, gonorrhoea, herpes or trichomoniasis are more susceptible to HIV. HIV positive individuals are highly susceptible to other infections, especially TB.

27.2 Deficiency diseases

These are caused by an unbalanced diet. See Chapter 12 on Human nutrition for symptoms of deficiency and food sources of vitamins and minerals.

Table 27.5 *Diseases from vitamin or mineral deficiencies*

Diseases	Vitamin or mineral deficient
Iron deficiency anaemia	Iron
Scurvy	Vitamin C
Night-blindness	Vitamin A
Rickets	Vitamin D

27.3 Physiological diseases

These are due to a malfunction in an organ or system of the body.

Cardiovascular disease

Deterioration of the heart and blood vessels leads to cardiovascular disease such as:
- **arteriosclerosis** – hardening of the arteries;
- **atherosclerosis** – accumulation of fatty material in the blood vessels;
- **coronary heart disease** – artery supplying blood to the heart muscle is blocked causing the heart to malfunction often resulting in a heart attack;
- **cerebral haemorrhage** or **stroke** – blood flow to brain is interrupted by a blockage or clot in a vessel.

Hypertension

Hypertension or high blood pressure shows no symptoms in its early stages and might go undetected until it results in heart failure, kidney failure or stroke. The following are known to contribute towards this condition:
1 **stress** – living conditions and job stress;
2 **obesity** – associated with diets rich in fats and carbohydrates; and
3 **oral contraceptives** – in some women.

Prevention seems to centre on the following:
1 **Exercise** regularly.
2 Maintain **weight** to correct level.

3 Eat **less salt** – body then retains less fluid.
4 **Reduce and manage stress**.
5 **Stop smoking**.

Diabetes mellitus

Diabetes mellitus or sugar diabetes is a decrease in the production of insulin from the pancreas or the production of non-functional insulin.

An immediate sign is that glucose appears in the urine. Normally all glucose filtered into the kidney tubule is reabsorbed, but in diabetes, glucose can be detected in urine. Individuals with this problem will also show symptoms including tiredness, weight loss and they could also lapse into a coma.

Like hypertension, it is a disease that can often be present without the condition being recognised by the individuals affected. Large-scale screening could be a method of detecting those suffering from the disease.

It cannot be cured, but all those who suffer can lead normal lives with the help of insulin or other medications, regular exercise, and management of diet.

Diabetes can lead to:
- **Eye disease and blindness** – Regular eye exams and timely treatment could prevent this.
- **Kidney disease** – Treatment to better control blood pressure and blood glucose levels is necessary.
- **Amputations** – Foot care programmes that include regular examinations and patient education could prevent these.
- **Cardiovascular disease** – Control blood pressure, blood glucose, and blood cholesterol levels.
- **Pregnancy complications** – Women and their babies have an increased risk for serious complications such as stillbirths, congenital malformations, and the need for Caesarean sections.
- **Complications from flu or pneumonia** – Diabetics are roughly three times more likely to die of these complications.

27.4 Hereditary diseases

These are passed on from parents to offspring often due to faulty genes – sickle cell disease and haemophilia are examples (see Chapter 25 on Genetics). Some cancers, and diabetes, can be due to faulty genes.

Down's syndrome is a chromosome abnormality, which results in mental retardation, heart defects, slightly slanted eyes and a short, stocky body. At meiosis chromosomes fail to separate fully so that a gamete with an extra chromosome 21 (n=24) is formed. At fertilisation this gamete fuses with a normal gamete (n=23). The zygote produced has 47 chromosomes in all its cells.

27.5 Social and economic implications of disease

International travel and trade facilitates the spread of disease and has a number of negative results that include the following:
- Economic damage to farmers in affected countries, since mortality rates are high and infected animals generally must be destroyed to prevent the spread of the disease. This adversely affects the overall process of economic development, leading to loss of employment, rising crime rate and extensive rural depopulation.
- A reduction in farm incomes as a result of losses in production and stock when farmers are forced to spend money and labour on their control.
- Restrictions in the trade of animals and animal products (meat, milk, hides) and on exports, which also leads to a loss of income.
- The risk of transmission of disease from animals to humans, e.g. TB, bird flu, or bovine spongiform encephalopathy ('Mad Cow' disease), which has lead to a reduction in the demand for beef in some countries.
- The HIV/AIDS epidemic contributes to rising health care costs and also a decline in productivity and economic development. Many new infections have been identified, particularly among young people in spite of attempts at public education. Individuals infected (or believed to be infected) by HIV have been rejected by their families, their loved ones and their communities.

Reversing the negative effect of disease on humans will involve:
- educating the public about basic nutrition, hygiene and responsible sexual behaviour to prevent infection with STIs;
- an emphasis on healthy lifestyles to include regular exercise, healthy diets and stress reduction, avoiding drug abuse and tobacco smoking; and
- improved sanitation to include the proper disposal of human waste and the provision of clean drinking water.

28 Psychological, social and economic effects of drug abuse

Any substance, which, when taken into the body, may modify one or more of the body's physical or mental functions is described as a **drug**.

Drug dependence (previously drug addiction) is described as the compulsion to take a drug, occasionally or continuously, to experience its mind altering effect or to avoid the discomfort produced by its absence.

28.1 Types of drugs

Alcohol is made by the fermentation process using many types of carbohydrates, e.g. from barley, grapes, potatoes and can be drunk in the form of beer, wine and alcoholic beverages.

Used in small amounts, it can remove inhibitions and produce talkativeness. Increased intake impairs the ability to concentrate ('if you drink don't drive'), causes forgetfulness, dulls mental activity, and leads eventually to slurred speech, inability to walk and total collapse.

Long-term consumption can result in permanent damage to the brain, increased blood pressure and heart rate, risk of stroke and heart failure. Alcohol abuse increases the risk of mouth and throat cancer, and can result in liver disease, damage to the digestive system, the pancreas and the kidneys.

The immune system can be suppressed, thus increasing the potential for illness.

Drinking during pregnancy raises the risk of low-birth weight babies. Heavy drinking during the early months of pregnancy can result in the birth of babies with foetal alcohol syndrome. These infants are likely to have small skulls, abnormal facial features, heart defects, retarded growth and mental development.

Marijuana is usually smoked in hand-made cigarettes; use is illegal in most countries. Its main mind-altering ingredient is **THC**.

Its effect on the body is to produce a pleasant, happy feeling together with dreams and distorted images. It often leads on to the use of other drugs such as cocaine.

Marijuana use reduces learning ability, limiting the capacity to absorb and retain information.

Persistent use can damage lungs and airways and raise the risk of cancer. Marijuana also affects hormones so that regular use can delay the onset of puberty in young men and reduce sperm production. For women, regular use may disrupt normal monthly menstrual cycles and inhibit ovulation. When pregnant women use marijuana, they run the risk of having smaller babies with lower birth weights, who are more likely than other babies to develop health problems.

Cocaine, an extract from leaves of the coca plant, is a stimulant. Initially, use reduces appetite and makes the user feel more alert, energetic, and self-confident – even more powerful. As the drug's effects wear off, a depression can set in, leaving the user feeling tired, agitated, fearful, and anxious.

Crack cocaine causes the heart to beat more rapidly and blood vessels to constrict. This results in the demand for a greater supply of blood. But the narrowed blood vessels are unable to deliver the volume of blood demanded, significantly increasing the risk of strokes.

Significant harm to foetuses of pregnant users can result. Foetal cocaine effects include miscarriage, premature labour, and low birth weight and head circumference at birth, greater chance of mental retardation and greater chance of developmental problems.

Promiscuous sexual activity is associated with the abuse of cocaine and so can increase the risk of HIV infection.

Ecstasy speeds up the nervous system and acts as a mood enhancer. Also referred to as 'the love drug', ecstasy often makes the user feel good, happy and relaxed – at least at first.

The effects include increased heart rate, body temperature, blood pressure and confidence, nausea, anxiety, feelings of well-being, sweating and loss of appetite. Users have also reported sleeplessness, anxiety, paranoia, problems concentrating and depression after taking the drug.

Physical problems that can occur are muscle tension, involuntary teeth-clenching, nausea, blurred vision, rapid eye movement, fever, chills or sweating.

Death often results from harmful overheating, or from drinking too much at one time and over stimulation of the nervous system resulting in heart attack or brain haemorrhage.

Nicotine first behaves like a stimulant and then as a depressant. It causes constriction of blood vessels in the skin, dilation of blood vessels in the muscles, increased heart rate and a rise in blood pressure.

Caffeine is found in tea, coffee, cola and cocoa. It removes feelings of tiredness, increases alertness and the ability to think clearly. Caffeine stimulates heart muscles and relaxes the muscles of the bronchioles. It can cause headaches, nervousness and dizziness.

Tranquilizers, such as Valium, produce drowsiness and can lead to long-term dependence.

Steroids are manufactured testosterone-like drugs that are usually taken to build muscle, enhance performance and improve appearance. While some steroids are used medically to treat many conditions including asthma, chronic lung disease, skin conditions and allergic reactions such as hives, abuse of steroids can have serious side effects.

Used correctly, steroids can increase muscle mass, strength, and endurance, but can also cause liver tumours, jaundice, water retention, and high blood pressure. Some users suffer from uncontrolled aggression and violent behaviour, severe mood swings, and depression. They often suffer from paranoid jealousy, extreme irritability and can have delusions.

A build-up of steroids in the body can lead to conditions such as hypertension, high cholesterol, kidney disease, stunted growth and heart damage. Women can experience irreversible deepening of the voice, shrinking of the breasts, menstrual irregularities, baldness and hair growth on other parts of the body. Men can experience baldness, breast enlargement, sterility, shrinking of testicles and impotence.

Antibiotics are drugs used for treating many serious and life-threatening bacterial infections. Frequent and inappropriate antibiotic use leads to the development of antibiotic-resistant bacteria requiring stronger and more costly medications to treat infections.

Because bacteria mutate much more quickly than researchers can develop new antibiotics, the possibility exists that soon highly lethal strains of resistant bacteria will evolve – and there won't be effective drugs to kill them.

Another consequence is the increased costs associated with prolonged illness.

28.2 Social and economic implications of drug abuse

Drug abuse has several effects not only on individuals but on their families, communities, workplaces and ultimately the country. These include:

- deterioration and breakdown of relationships with family, friends, and co-workers;
- suicide;
- susceptibility to mental illness, cardiovascular disease, respiratory disorders, cancer and sexually transmitted infections;
- absenteeism and a decline in productivity in the workplace;
- violent crime and criminal activity – including theft and fraud;
- domestic violence;
- abuse of spouse and children;
- neglect of children;
- accidents at home, on the road and in the workplace;
- increased promiscuity and so transmission of sexually transmitted infections;
- poverty;
- corruption of the justice system and government;
- increased cost of policing and of security measures to crack down on the trade; and
- inconvenience of security measures to law-abiding citizens.

Index

inflorescence, 23, 24 & *ill.*
ingestion, 31
insect pollination, 23–24 & *ill.*
intrauterine contraceptive device
    (IUCD/IUD), 63–64 & *ill.*
invertebrates
    responses to stimuli, 50–51 & *ill.*
involuntary muscles, 49
iron and steel, 17–18
irrigation, 18
Islets of Langerhans, 57 *tab.*
isotonic solution, 21

J
joints, 49 & *ill.*

K
kidneys, 44–45 & *ill.*
    failure, 46
kingdoms, 5 & *ill.*

L
lacto/lacto-ovo vegetarians, 34
lamellae, 37
larynx, 38 & *ill.*
learning methods, 1
leaves
    adaptations for photosynthesis, 28–29
    structure, 28 & *ill.*
length (definition), 59
lens, 54–55 & *ill.*
levels of organisation, 20 & *tab.*, 21
ligaments, 49
light intensity, 10, 29
limbs, 48 & *ill.*
limiting factors, 14
line transect, 12 & *ill.*
Linnaeus, Carolus, 5
lipase, 32
    optimum pH level, 22
liver, 44
living organisms, characteristics, 19
locomotion, 19
loop of Henlé, 45
lungs, 44
lymphatic vessels, 41

M
malnutrition, 34
maltase, 32
mammals
    body temperature regulation, 55–56
    excretion, 44
    gas exchange mechanisms, 38 & *ill.*
    growth, 59 & *ill.*
mango *(Mangifera)*, 26 *ill.*
marijuana, 80
marine pollution, 16
mass, 58–59
maturity, 19
mechanical digestion, 31
medulla oblongata, 52 & *ill.*
meiosis, 60, 67 & *ill.*
    compared to mitosis, 68 *tab.*
melanin (definition), 69

melanocytes (definition), 69
meninges, 51
menstruation, 60
meristems, 25
metabolism, 22
    human, 57 *tab.*
    plants, 29
micropyle, 24
minerals, 34–35 & *tab.*, 78 & *tab.*
    in plant metabolism, 29 *tab.*
mitochondria, 20
mitosis, 26, 66 & *ill.*
    compared to meiosis, 68 *tab.*
molars, 31 & *ill.*
molecules, 20
mosquitoes, 76–77 & *ill.*
movement, 19
muscles, 47, 49 & *ill.*
mutualism (definition), 7

N
natural classification, 5 & *ill.*
natural immunity, 77–78 & *tab.*
natural selection, 74
natural/rhythm contraception method, 64
    & *ill.*
negative feedback in homeostasis, 45
nephrons, 45 & *ill.*
nervous system, 51–53 & *ill.*
nets for sampling, 12 & *ill.*
neurones, 51–52 & *ill.*
newspapers, 17
niche, 10
nicotine, 38, 80–81
nitrogen cycle, 8 & *ill.*
nitrogen-fixing bacteria, 6, 8 & *ill.*
non-renewable resources, 17–18
nuclear power, 18
nucleus, 20
number (definition), 59
nutrient cycling, 8–9 & *ill.*
nutrition (definition), 19
    human, 31 & *ill.*

O
obesity, 35
oesophagus, 31, 32 *ill.*
oil, 16
omnivores (definition), 6, 31
optimum temperature, 22
orders, 5 & *ill.*
organelles, 20
organisms
    relationships, 6–7
organs, 21
osmoregulation, 45
osmosis, 21
outbreeding, 74
ovary, 23 & *ill.*, 24, 57 *tab.*
ovule, 24
ovum, 60–61 & *ill.*
oxygen, 44
ozone layer, 15

P
pancreatic juice, 32
parasitic organisms (definition), 6
parasitism (definition), 7
pathogenic diseases, 76–78 & *tab.*
pectoral girdle, 48
pedicel, 23
pedigree charts, 72
pelvic girdle, 48
pentadactyl plan, 48 & *ill.*
peppered moth *(Biston betularia)*, 74
pepsin
    optimum pH level, 22
perianth, 23 & *ill.*
pericarp, 24
peripheral nervous system, 52–53 & *ill.*
pests, biological control of, 18
petals, 23 & *ill.*
pH, effect on enzyme activity, 22 & *ill.*
pharynx, 38 & *ill.*
phenotype (definition), 68, 69
phenotypic differences, 73 & *ill.*
phloem, 40 & *ill.*
photoautotrophs, 5
photosynthesis, 9, 28–29
    flowering plants, 37
phototaxis, 50
phototropism, 50, 51 & *ill.*
phyla, 5 & *ill.*
physical/barrier contraception methods,
    63–64 & *ill.*
physiological diseases, 78–79
pistil, 23 & *ill.*
pituitary gland, 46, 57 *tab.*, 62
placenta, 61 & *ill.*
plants, 5
    and animal interdependence, 9
    comparison of plant/animal cells, 20 *ill.*
    differences from animals, 19–20 & *tab.*
    excretory products, 44
    food storage, 43 & *tab.*
    reproduction, 23–27 & *ill.*
    respiration, 37
    sampling techniques, 12 & *ill.*
    tropic movements/tropisms, 47 & *tab.*,
        50
    water conservation, 44
    see also vascular plants
plasma, 41
plasma membrane, 20
plasmolysed cells, 21 & *ill.*, 40
plastics, 17
platelets, 42
plumule, 25 & *ill.*
poikilothermic animals, 55
polled animals, 73
pollen, 23–24
pollen tube, 24
pollination, 23–24 & *ill.*
pollution, 15–17
pooter, 13 & *ill.*
populations, 10, 14
    estimates of size, 13
positive feedback in homeostasis, 45
predator-prey relationship, 14